LEST
WE FORGET

LEST
WE FORGET

REMEMBRANCE & COMMEMORATION

EDITED BY MAGGIE ANDREWS

WITH CHARLES BAGOT JEWITT & NIGEL HUNT

First published 2011

The History Press
The Mill, Brimscombe Port
Stroud, Gloucestershire, GL5 2QG
www.thehistorypress.co.uk

British Library Cataloguing in Publication Data.
A catalogue record for this book is available from the British Library.

ISBN 978 0 7524 5965 3

Typesetting and origination by The History Press
Printed in Great Britain
Manufacturing managed by Jellyfish Print Solution Ltd

CONTENTS

LIST OF CONTRIBUTORS

Dr Maggie Andrews: Assistant Head (Undergraduate Programmes), Institute of
    Humanities and Creative Arts, University of Worcester
Commander Charles Bagot Jewitt: Chief Executive, National Memorial
    Arboretum, Alrewas, Staffordshire
Dr Karen Burnell: Research Associate, Department of Mental Health Sciences,
    University College London
Dr Bob Bushaway: Former Director of Research and Enterprise Services
    and Honorary Research Fellow at the Centre for First World War Studies,
    University of Birmingham
Kristýna Bušková: Graduate student, Institute of Work, Health and
    Organisations, University of Nottingham
Dr Fan Carter: Principal Lecturer in Media and Cultural Studies, Kingston
    University
Dr Jamie Cleland: Senior Lecturer in Sports Sociology, Staffordshire University
Dr Peter Donaldson: Lecturer in History, University of Kent
Dr M.K. Flynn: Senior Lecturer, International Politics, University of the West of
    England
Dr Jane Gledhill: Independent Scholar and Lecturer in Christian Spirituality,
    Sarum College
Professor Paul Gough: Pro Vice Chancellor and Executive Dean of the Faculty
    of Creative Arts, University of the West of England
Professor Hilary J. Grainger: Dean, London College of Fashion, University of
    the Arts London
Professor Susan-Mary Grant: Professor of American History, Newcastle
    University
Professor Keith Grieves: School of Education, Kingston University

Foreword

'LEST WE FORGET'

Remembrance Sunday and Armistice Day ceremonies have, over the past decade, been growing once more in significance as public events; and war memorials remain a key element of the landscape of many of our cities, towns and villages. However, the forms and practices of commemoration change as society evolves. Elements of informality now feature in acts of remembrance which would have been unthinkable in earlier generations and private grief is more on display. There is a hugely increased role for broadcast and the internet. Museum exhibitions also are reflecting an increased interest in memory, pilgrimage and contemporary heritage; and memorials are being placed in new physical spaces, constructed from modern materials in ways that challenge and provoke.

Remembrance, in terms of acts of commemoration and memorialisation of those who have died in the service of their country, is thus a legitimate area for study and re-interpretation in the context of the UK and the modern world. All traditional assumptions about national identity, including remembrance, must be regularly re-examined in the context of our multicultural society and in an ever-changing political climate. We also need to be aware that most people in today's diverse society have not shared the experience of national war beyond the popular representations in film and museums.

The Royal British Legion, now in its ninetieth year, is proud to act as the 'National Custodian of Remembrance' and will always maintain the focus for Remembrance Sunday and Armistice Day on the armed forces. However, The Royal British Legion is very much part of the changing world and seeks to keep the concept of remembrance strong and relevant to all. At the Legion's year-round centre for remembrance, the National Memorial Arboretum in Staffordshire, not only are the fallen honoured, but also those who have served and suffered for the whole national community, including family members and comrades of the bereaved. Quiet pride, in no way jingoistic, is fostered in those who have given our country so much, and in so many ways.

In 2008, in this context, The Royal British Legion, the National Memorial Arboretum and the universities of Staffordshire and Nottingham set up a series of seminars to:

- deepen understanding of the meaning and significance of commemoration in the contemporary culture informed by a study of the practice of commemoration in other times and cultures
- inform the practice of commemoration and remembrance for future generations
- explore the relationship between remembrance, commemoration and the armed forces covenant
- stimulate further study of remembrance, commemoration and memorials

Drawing on an inter-disciplinary group of experts working in the fields of History and Heritage, International Relations and Politics, Psychology, Architecture, Human Geography, Media and the Creative Arts, the study of religions and teacher training alongside practitioners working for religious groups, in the armed forces, education, the Mass Observation Archive, The Royal British Legion and at the National Memorial Arboretum, the seminars have so far produced a website, a dedicated journal edition of *War and Conflict Studies* and this volume.

The topics covered by the articles in the book are eclectic, and deliberately so, because only by reading widely around the subject can we understand developing trends and appreciate the rightful place of remembrance in our contemporary, globalised world. If you are interested in any of the many facets of remembrance, then I commend this book to you.

Lieutenant General Sir John Kiszely, KCB, MC
National President, The Royal British Legion

The editors of this book would like to express their thanks to:

Professor Christine King, for inspiring the concept and all those who participated in the NMA Seminars on Remembrance Commemoration and Memorials; The Royal British Legion, especially John Farmer, National Chairman, Chris Simpkins, Director General, and Stuart Gendall, Director of Communications, for their support of the seminars and this book; Dave Faul for his technical expertise.

Introduction

UNPICKING SOME THREADS OF REMEMBRANCE

Charles Bagot Jewitt

How does traditional 'Remembrance' relate to core human emotions? Do the enormous number of memorials throughout Britain indicate that remembrance is part of the universality of the human spirit or are they a purely western cultural phenomenon? These were typical of the questions underlying our seminar discussions at the National Memorial Arboretum and at The Royal British Legion Head Office at Haig House in London. Not all questions could be answered but the multi-disciplinary approach adopted through our seminar series shed some interesting new light on the contrasting motivations for acts of remembrance and memorialisation. The threads explored will become more apparent as you read through the various articles in the volume.

State, or 'top down', motivation is the key driver in national remembrance. Many nation states wish to be seen as recognising their role in the loss of their individual citizens in conflict, and many governments play a part in a national commemoration and memorialisation process. In a British military context this can be viewed as the state fulfilling part of its 'Military Covenant' in formally recognising loss and grief. State memorials are often significant architectural structures, and their sites can be the focus for significant national commemorative events, such as Memorial Day and Veterans Day at Arlington National Cemetery in the USA, or Remembrance Sunday at the Cenotaph in London.

The Menin Gate at Ypres, Belgium, designed by Blomfield, and Thiepval Memorial in northern France, designed by Lutyens, are state-scale memorials which provide similar iconic recognition to the British missing of First World War battlefields. Other such memorials, including Vimy Ridge, Canada's

Fig. 1 Armed Forces Memorial at the National Memorial Arboretum, Staffordshire, in the snow.

Fig. 2 Basra Wall at the National Memorial Arboretum, Staffordshire.

impressive memorial to the First World War in northern France, and indeed the Cenotaph, do not contain the names of those who are being commemorated. By contrast, the UK's new Armed Forces Memorial at the National Memorial Arboretum lists nearly 16,000 names that have died on duty in the military service of the country since 1945 and is, arguably, becoming something of a contemporary shrine.

While state-sponsored sites and ceremonies are needed, they are clearly not enough and for many smaller communities comradeship driven from the heart of the community (or 'bottom up') is the motivation for acts of remembrance, and for both formal and informal memorialisation. The town and village war memorials placed in nearly every significant community of the United Kingdom after the First World War, and added to after the Second, are often kept up to date in the present time (see Chapter 22). These still provide a setting for acts of remembrance similar in form to the national events at the Cenotaph. However, unlike some state memorials, the inclusion of names is critical in representing people who were intimately known to their communities and whose loss has been keenly felt.

The vast growth of websites to individuals lost in Afghanistan, including Google Earth's 'map the fallen' project which was created by a company engineer in his spare time, may be considered as another form of 'bottom-up' response to recognising the deaths of individuals in an increasingly global community. In very similar fashion, Anfield football stadium in Liverpool provided the setting for a huge but very informal outpouring of non-military grief after the Hillsborough Disaster in 1989 (see Chapter 9), and today the dead are commemorated by both a traditional memorial and an online section of the club's website in the way of many contemporary deaths on the battlefield.

The Basra Memorial Wall is a contemporary example of how, from informal beginnings, comradeship memorials can quickly become formalised. Brass plaques started appearing in Basra from 2003 onwards where individual British and coalition soldiers fell, and an initiative from a Roman Catholic chaplain resulted in a wall being built outside their headquarters. The wall then became the icon for the British presence in Basra and a centrepiece for the formal British withdrawal ceremonies from the province, which were watched on television worldwide. After a campaign by parents of the deceased, the memorial was rebuilt in the National Memorial Arboretum and dedicated in a ceremony attended by the leaders of the three main British political parties in March 2010.

Many memorials become sites of pilgrimage, and often these are memorials placed on sites of relevance to specific conflicts or incidents (see Chapter 13). A substantial memorial can be an important feature of a preserved battlefield, such as at Waterloo where the dramatic Lion Mound overlooks the entire site; or at the site of a human catastrophe, such as at Ground Zero in New York. Some of the oldest memorials in the United Kingdom were both places of faith pilgrimages and served a commemorative function: Battle Abbey, which

Fig. 3 The Polish Armed Forces Memorial at the National Memorial Arboretum.

Fig. 4 The Shot at Dawn Memorial at the National Memorial Arboretum, Staffordshire.

Fig. 5 Mother and child mourn at the National Memorial Arboretum, Staffordshire.

commemorates the Battle of Hastings in Sussex, was founded no later than 1070 and is thus almost certainly the earliest battlefield site memorial still in exist- ence in the country. Another early example is the stunning Crecy memorial window in Gloucester cathedral, paid for by a knight after the famous battle in 1346. Large-scale military campaigns such as Gallipoli spawned a variety of bat- tlefield memorials on the peninsula created for differing purposes (see Chapter 2) and also memorials far removed from the events, including at the National Memorial Arboretum where a memorial makes a valuable link to the Turkish battlefield and is a useful educational tool.

Recognition, particularly for those who feel that their contribution has been 'hidden from history', provides another motivation for commemoration. Memorials of recognition to particular groups often form the focus for 'tribal' gatherings. Arguably, acts of remembrance at such memorials thinly disguise the primary purpose of re-union and the memorials themselves usually do not contain names of the fallen, although they may contain listings of campaigns, military honours or mottos. Such memorials may even be placed by nation states in other countries, where the message 'don't forget us, we helped you' is implicit. Striking artistic form can be an important component of such memorials, as in those of Australia, New Zealand and Canada now located in London's parks, which celebrate the contribution of those countries to freedom in Britain in the World Wars. Not infrequently, such memorials may be dedicated many years after the events they commemorate; the London Australian Memorial was dedicated as late as 2003.

Similarly, the Polish Armed Forces Memorial, dedicated at the National Memorial Arboretum in 2009, was initiated by the children of combatants in the Second World War. It deliberately tells the story of their parents' contribution to the British and Allied war effort in an attempt to 'right the wrong' when Polish servicemen were not allowed to take part on the victory parades for fear of antagonising Stalin's Soviet Union. Another comradeship-inspired Polish War Memorial listing the names of the fallen has already existed for many years in Northolt, London. Many other memorials at the National Memorial Arboretum share similar motivational reasons and some have been dedicated by non-military organisations such as police, fire and ambulance services, or national charities with a reason for commemoration such as the Royal National Lifeboat Institution.

Monuments put up by groups (or 'tribes') to remember specific individuals, perhaps especially to the 'great and the good', can be seen in a similar light. It may be argued that by placing a memorial to a leading individual, such as Admiral Lord Nelson after the Battle of Trafalgar or to Air Chief Marshal Sir Keith Park in London 2010, the 'tribes' are indulging in a celebrity culture or even creating a secular sainthood, where the individual is seen as the manifestation of the group. It may also be significant that those who have personal or close family associations with the honoured individual are gathering to themselves a sense of distinction by association. However, individual memorialisation should also be recognised as being as old as mankind and fundamental to the human condition, as a look at some of the amazing medieval tombs and chantry chapels in Britain's ancient cathedrals and churches, where sometimes priests were paid to say mass for souls of the wealthy departed in 'perpetuity', quickly confirms.

The emotive nature of remembrance may lead to acts of remembrance and memorial sites becoming highly contentious. The Northern Ireland 'marching season' is an example of where acts of remembrance still have the capacity to inflame. Dr Flynn's article on Long Kesh (see Chapter 20) shows how both Protestant and Catholic factions, both of which were represented in the prison population, now vie for their version of history to be immortalised on the site. Other memorials, designed for non-controversial purposes, such as to Sir Arthur 'Bomber' Harris outside St Clement Danes in London, have found themselves becoming contested space because of the popular legacy, and in some eyes infamy, of the individual concerned. The memorial was subject to a protest by the Peace Pledge Union at its dedication by Her Majesty the Queen Mother in 1992.

Some memorials may be deeply political, by their construction setting out deliberately to contest a point or to drive forward an agenda, occasionally attracting wide media coverage. The Shot at Dawn Memorial in the National Memorial Arboretum, one of many memorials to perceived abuse, was put in place to press the case for a pardon for servicemen executed during the First World War. Pardon was eventually achieved by an amendment to the Armed Forces Act in August 2006, by which time the *Daily Telegraph* had run a photograph of the memorial across its front page. Similarly, the British Nuclear Test Veterans Memorial nearby almost invariably attracts media attention when acts of commemoration are held due to the contestation surrounding the effects on those who took part and their offspring. A resin edition of a statue called 'The Abandoned Soldier' by James Napier was raised in Trafalgar Square in May 2007 as part of a plan to draw the government's attention to the plight of those suffering mental injury due to military service. The sculpture has still not been created in its final form, yet the concept alone has the capacity to draw press and political attention to the cause it represents.

Remembrance is full of contrasting motivations, and frequently many contradictions. Often, elements of acts of remembrance or memorialisation contain more than one of the elements described above. Much of the primary motivation to remember, of course, reflects humankind's deep and universal desire for significance, possibly immortality, and this is true in every age and culture. However, remembrance as the concept we think about today, be it narrowly focused on the military or more widely focused on different segments of the population, is ultimately a reaction felt by 'survivors' whenever life is cut short, and for whatever reason. Often remembrance brings with it other deep feelings of shock, anger and grief, and attempts to harness these and make sense of *Homo sapiens*' periodic inhumanity to his fellow creatures. The laudable desire is never to repeat the mistakes of the past, and to preserve the memory of the fallen 'lest we forget'.

Contesting Cultures of Remembrance

USUALLY, a degree of consensus exists in the decision to site a memorial and in the formation of acts of commemoration. However, with the passage of time and reinterpretation of history, subsequent contestation of memorials and rituals which were at one time widely embraced can occur. This is demonstrated in chapters on commemoration of the Second Boer War and Gallipoli. That said, some cultures of remembrance have been deliberately fostered to provoke or to alter a narrative of history, often for political ends. This is exemplified by the chapter on slave memorials.

One

REMEMBERING THE DEAD, FORGIVING THE ENEMY:
THE ROYAL ENGINEERS & THE COMMEMORATION OF THE SECOND BOER WAR

Dr Peter Donaldson

The unveiling of the Royal Engineers' memorial arch to the fallen of the Second Boer War at the corps' headquarters at Brompton Barracks, Chatham, on 26 July 1905 was greeted with all the pomp and circumstance that one would expect of such an important national ritual in Edwardian England. With the king in attendance to perform the official dedication, the *Chatham News* vividly captured the sense of collective pride that singled the day out as a patriotic carnival: 'Flags! Flags! Flags! Flags here, flags there, flags everywhere – nothing but flags of all colours, all sizes and all descriptions, the whole combining to make a bright display.'[1]

Yet such nationalistic unanimity masked the difficulties that the corps' memorial committee had faced as it had attempted to construct a memory site in honour of the 431 Royal Engineers who had died in the war. Although the scheme had been instigated by no less a person than Lord Kitchener, himself a Royal Engineer and latterly commander-in-chief of the British forces in South Africa, the memory of the war and the nature of the proposal were sufficiently contentious to negate the deference that seniority would normally command.

In May 1902, Kitchener, who had been commissioned into the Royal Engineers in 1871, had written to the commandant of the corps at Chatham, Sir T. Fraser, with the offer of 'four bronze statues of Boers and four bas-reliefs for use in a war memorial to the fallen'.[2] For good measure he had enclosed a detailed sketch of his proposal. Unsurprisingly, Fraser had been quick to accept the offer and a memorial committee meeting in October 1902, chaired by Sir Robert Harrison, the Inspector General of Fortifications, unanimously agreed to press ahead with the plan.

Fig. 1 The original sketch plan for
the Kruger Memorial.

However, notwithstanding this official seal of approval from the senior commanders, the scheme soon ran into trouble. The Boer statues and bas-reliefs had
originally been intended as the focal points for a monument in honour of Paul
Kruger, the former President of the Transvaal. The pieces had been embargoed at
the outbreak of war and eventually donated to Kitchener who, as we have seen
above, subsequently offered them to the Royal Engineers' memorial committee.
Although, in many ways, Kitchener's offer can be securely sited in the classic
tradition of the triumphal, the contentious symbolism of the statuary must have
rung some alarm bells even with the original memorial committee members.

Indeed, the committee's appreciation of the sensitive nature of the proposal
can be discerned from their immediate response. Despite insisting that the pieces
should be viewed as 'impersonal' and 'works of art', they nevertheless decided
that a bas-relief depicting the peace conference at McNeill's farm after the British
army's ignominious defeat at the Battle of Majuba Hill in the First Boer War was
a step too far, and should be replaced by a 'plaque recording Lord Kitchener's gift
of the bronzes'.[3] This nod towards conciliation would, however, prove to be far
less than was going to be necessary to stem the tide of criticism that the committee would eventually face over the inclusion of such controversial images.

Fig. 2 One of the
Boer figures donated
by Kitchener.

For many in Britain, and certainly for a sizeable proportion of those who had
fought in the war, anti-Boer feeling, which was an inevitable consequence of
the brutality of the conflict for British combatants and which had been fuelled
domestically by the 'yellow press', sat uneasily with the assimilation of the Boer
Republics into a federated British South Africa by the Treaty of Vereeniging.[4] It
could, therefore, hardly have come as a surprise to the memorial committee that,
when details of the proposed scheme were announced in the corps' magazine,
it was quickly swamped by a flood of complaints. It was, however, only when
Field Marshal Sir John Simmons, former Inspector-General of Fortifications
from 1875–80 and Governor of Malta until his retirement in 1888, put his weight
behind the opposition that the committee eventually caved in and resolved 'to
defer any further action until a General Meeting of the corps can be held'.[5]

Although nearly all those present at the corps' general meeting on 6 June 1903 were in agreement that the original plans of the memorial committee to accept the Boer statues and bas-reliefs should be rescinded, there were still heated exchanges when it came to providing a rationale for this decision. Major M. Hildebrand, a retired Royal Engineers officer, clearly articulated the view that consideration of Boer sensibilities had to take precedence when it came to commemorating the war. In a letter sent to the editor of the Royal Engineers' journal and read out at the meeting, he made plain that pressing ahead with the original plan would, in his view, 'cause the keenest feeling of resentment amongst our new fellow subjects'.[6]

Major-General Sir Elliott Wood, who had served as engineer-in-chief during the war and was a member of the original memorial committee, was quick to voice his support for this line of reasoning. Having been responsible for drawing up the original sketch-plan of Kitchener's scheme, he was clearly keen to distance himself from what had turned out to be a contentious and manifestly unpopular proposal. The choice of design was, he insisted, 'a very important question … for it might become more than a corps' matter; it might go beyond this and affect the army and perhaps the country generally, if we were to give offence to our new fellow subjects'.

For two retired senior officers, however, the memory of the human cost of the recent fighting was still too fresh for consideration of such political niceties to take priority. Arguing that it was first important 'to clear up our own views before we consider those of other people', Lieutenant-General Sir Robert Grant urged those assembled to 'remember that it was through what we hold to be [the Boers'] mistaken views and their mistaken actions that we lost the officers and men to whom we wish to erect the memorial'. General Sir James Browne, a former colonel commandant of the corps, was prepared to go one step further when apportioning blame. In a letter read out at the meeting on his behalf, he maintained that to use such 'undesirable images would be a monument to bad taste, never to be effaced', for the statues 'were made to honour Mr. Kruger, the man of all others in this world responsible for the deaths of those we wish to honour'.

An interesting argument to bolster further the case against the original proposal was presented by Sir Thomas Gallway, who had recently succeeded Sir Richard Harrison as Inspector-General of Fortifications. Insisting that the minutes should record his 'strong protest' against Kitchener's scheme on the grounds that the statues 'represent an armed enemy', Gallway raised the moral stakes by arguing that, before any decision could be reached, the meeting must first 'consider the feelings of the relatives of our gallant dead'. Major J. Winn, a member of the original war memorial committee, although differing on the nature of the views held by the bereaved, was still equally adamant that they merited special consideration. His attitude had, he said, 'hardened' against using the statues as the result of a letter he had recently received from the father of one of the fallen: 'He thought that, if the Boers would consider it to be a bad thing for the figures to be used, it ought not to be done. Knowing that this man lost a son in the war, I feel more strongly that his views should carry weight on the subject.'[7]

With no one able or willing to speak out in support of the original plan, the meeting unanimously resolved to elect a new committee with instructions to start the process afresh. The threat of any further dissent was subsequently averted by devolving the question of form to the professional care of an established architect, Ingress Bell. His decision to opt for a triumphal arch, to mirror the Crimean Arch erected at the corps' headquarters in Brompton in the 1860s, was reassuringly uncontroversial and the project proceeded to completion without further hitches. The Boer statues were relegated to a far-flung corner of the parade ground in Brompton Barracks to ensure the memorial should remain unsullied by any symbolic association.

An interesting footnote to this contentious issue occurred fifteen years after the unveiling of the memorial arch. A decision by the South African government to proceed, somewhat belatedly, with the construction of the Kruger memorial in Pretoria once again brought the political significance of the Boer statues into high relief. In December 1920, General Jan Smuts, the South African Prime Minister and former Boer guerrilla commander, approached his old adversary Alfred Milner, the Secretary of State for the colonies, requesting the return of the statues. Before Milner could accede to the request, he first had to seek permission from the Royal Engineers, who retained ownership of two of the statues, and Kitchener's son, who had removed the other two figures to the Kitchener residence in Broome Park. Having received no objection from either party, in March 1921 the statues were returned for, in Milner's words, 'political reasons as an act of goodwill'.[8] All four statues can now be found adorning the plinth of the Kruger memorial in Church Square, Pretoria.

Notes

1 *Chatham News*, 29 July 1905.

2 Royal Engineers Museum (REM), RO270, Royal Engineers War Memorial Committee, minutes, 19 December 1902.

3 REM, RO270, Royal Engineers War Memorial Committee, minutes, 24 October 1902. The Battle of Majuba Hill, 27 February 1881, was a decisive defeat for the British in the First Boer War. See Ian Castle, *Majuba 1881; the Hill of Destiny* (Colchester: Osprey, 1996).

4 See Bill Nasson, *The South African War 1899–1902* (London: Arnold, 1999), pp. 227–33.

5 REM, RO270, Royal Engineers War Memorial Committee, minutes, 19 November 1902.

6 REM, RO270, letter from Major Hildebrand to Royal Engineers War Memorial Committee, undated.

7 REM, RO270, Royal Engineers War Memorial Committee, minutes, 6 June 1903.

8 REM, *The Sapper*, Vol. 26, No 307, February 1921, p. 99.

Two

THE MEMORIALISATION OF GALLIPOLI AND THE DARDANELLES 1915:

History & Meaning

Dr Bob Bushaway

Unscathed, exulting in the amber light,
We left behind the immemorial Cape.

'The Sentinel', Geoffrey Dearmer (1918)

The process of establishing a landscape of memory in the systematic memori-alisation of the battlefields of Gallipoli and the Dardanelles – the scene of bitter fighting and trench warfare in 1915 – has been continuous since military and naval operations ended. At the southern tip of the European Peninsula, forming part of the Turkish province of Canakkale, known to the Entente powers during the First World War as Gallipoli, is the European bank to the narrow seaway of the Dardanelles which links the Mediterranean to the Black Sea and has long been seen as the strategic key to the control of the eastern Mediterranean and Black Sea approaches to Asia. Both the early memorials and the cemeteries of the dead were made where the soldiers fought and died across a field of con-flict whose dimensions were considerably constrained by the conditions of fixed field fortifications and static warfare. Since 1915, and in marked contrast to other First World War battlefields in Europe, both the victors and the defeated have striven to memorialise the area.[1] Undoubtedly a tactical, operational and stra-tegic defeat for the Entente powers, and a clear local victory for the Ottoman Empire under the control of the group of revolutionary army officers known as the 'Young Turks', with the help of their German allies, by November 1918 the Ottoman Empire had been defeated. The first wave of memorialisation took place between 1919 and 1925 – the tenth anniversary of the beginning of the

Fig. 1 Turkish memorial to the shore batteries which defended the Dardanelles against the attempted naval incursion of 18 March 1915.

land campaign. On returning to the peninsula, initially as an army of occupation, the victorious Allies created their own landscape of memory. In the words of T.J. Pemberton, who recorded their work: 'Before the war had come to an end the Governments of the Empire had decided that the name of every man and woman who had made the supreme sacrifice on the battlefields and oceans of the world for Britain's cause should be commemorated in a lasting monument.'[2]

The Ottoman sultanate was overthrown, the original Treaty of Sevres (1919) was rejected and, after the Greek–Turkish War, was replaced by the Treaty of Lausanne (1923), and the new Republic of Turkey was proclaimed on 29 October 1923 with its capital at Ankara and Mustafa Kemal as the Republic's first president.

Pemberton recorded at the time that 'The Turks, whose dead lie in Gallipoli soil in equal numbers to their erstwhile enemies, have made no attempt whatever to mark their places of burial'. He comments that in only one place, at the Nek, was there evidence of Turkish memorialisation in the form of 'a pyramidal block of concrete, surmounted by five live shells and standing only some fifteen feet in height'. He continues: 'The Turks raised no other memorial to their dead. Here and there are to be found Turkish cemeteries, but they are not marked nor intended to be remembered.'[3]

In 1922 the Greek army was defeated in the Greek–Turkish War. The Greek agricultural population was removed to Thrace, Salonika and Athens to be replaced steadily by Turkish communities. Turkish memorialisation, partly in reflection of the national secular characteristics of the new Republic and partly to glorify the achievements of Mustafa Kemal (Kemal Ataturk), whose own deeds in no small way brought about the victory at Gallipoli and the birth of the modern Turkish Republic, marks the first phase of Turkish commemoration. Since then, successive phases of Turkish memorialisation have emphasised the role of Turkey's armed forces in defending both Turkish sovereignty under the secular constitution of 1923, and the neutrality of the Dardanelles in the latter period as a NATO ally during the years of the Cold War. As a result, the landscape of memory has been given new and different meanings relating to Turkish independence rarely accessible to non-Turkish visitors. Meaning is not fixed and although reconciliation has become an overarching and symbolic meaning for the transformed landscape, each period and the initial allied stage reveals contested meanings which continue into the twenty-first century.

The imperatives of the national, democratic, secular and socialist new Republic of Turkey are proclaimed as much by the Turkish memorialisation of Gallipoli as through the nationwide cult of Kemal Ataturk, which has so far defined modern Turkey and its post-Ottoman national sovereignty. Between November 1919 and Pemberton's account in 1928, the Imperial (now Commonwealth) War Graves Commission had constructed an intricate landscape consisting of thirty-one cemeteries containing over 19,000 graves. The majority of these cemeteries were designed by Sir John Burnet. Headstones take the form of plaques raised

Fig. 2 Australian memorial, Lone Pine Cemetery.

at an angle from the ground and large cemeteries include the Great Stone of Remembrance and the Cross cut into a flat stone as part of the embankment. Six memorials to the missing, on which were carved the names of over 27,000 soldiers, sailors and airmen for whom there was no known grave on the peninsula, were erected at Cape Helles, together with separate memorials to the missing in the Anzac area at Lone Pine (Australia) and at Twelve Tree Copse, Chunuk Bair and at Hill Sixty (New Zealand). A separate cemetery and ossuary were erected by the French at Morto Bay to commemorate their forces during the campaign, and was inaugurated on 9 June 1930.

The Entente mythos for Gallipoli and the Dardanelles in 1915 is a narrative of close-run events ending in ultimate defeat. Numerous accounts in the English language historiography, beginning with the Report of the Dardanelles Commission to Parliament in 1917, have concluded that the campaign was boldly

Fig. 3 Chunuk Bair, New Zealand memorial for the missing.

conceived and bravely executed, resulting in a narrow but honourable defeat. The Turkish mythos links the victory to the formation of the modern Republic, in which a successful defence of the Turkish homeland from amphibious assault, conducted through the skill of Turkish and German leadership and the bravery of Turkish forces drawn from across the entire Ottoman Empire, had resulted in a new beginning for the Republic of Turkey, captured by Mustafa Kemal's words: 'Peace at home, peace in the world.' Turkish memorialisation at Gallipoli therefore faces the future rather than the past.

Between the birth of the Republic in 1923 and the death of Ataturk in 1938, the landscape of the peninsula was laid out with a series of pedagogic plaques which marked the decisive points where the landings or the subsequent thrusts inland were blocked by Turkish troops. Ataturk's presence on the peninsula in 1915 was also marked by a series of dramatic statues of the president at different

Fig. 4 Bas-relief applied to the face of the Turkish Martyrs' Memorial depicting a bayonet charge.

points in the campaign. Conscious of the need for reconciliation and recognising the nationalist aspirations of Australia and New Zealand during the 1930s, Ataturk wrote a message to Australian mothers, which is now widely proclaimed at different places in the landscape:

> Those heroes who shed their blood and lost their lives ... are now lying in the soil of a friendly country. Therefore rest in peace ... You, the mothers, who sent their sons from faraway countries, wipe away your tears. Your sons are now lying in our bosom and are in peace. After having lost their lives on this land they have become our sons as well.[4]

This is a different message from the one which is proclaimed on the hillside above Kilitbahir at the Narrows on the European bank of the Dardanelles. There, a Turkish soldier proclaims: 'Traveller, halt! The soil you tread once witnessed the end of an era. Listen, in this quiet mound there once beat the heart of a nation.' These words commemorate the naval fighting on 18 March 1915 when the attempt to force their way up the Straits of the Dardanelles was defeated by Turkish shore batteries and mines.

Between 1936 and 1952 the Republic of Turkey defended the neutrality of the Dardanelles seaway, firstly under the terms of the Montreux Convention (1936), then during the Second World War, when Turkey proclaimed her continuing neutrality until declaring war on Germany in the last days of the fighting, and again in 1952 when Turkey became a member of NATO. New defences were constructed during this period in order to protect the straits. Turkish memorialisation punctuates this period and glorifies the deeds of the army during the fighting;

thus the memorial to Lieutenant-General Nuri Yamut, the commanding officer of the Second Corps, was dedicated in 1942 and commemorates the estimated 10,000 Turkish soldiers who died at Zigin Dere (Gully Ravine). The memorial at the Turkish military port of Akbas Bay was made in 1946, and the Sargiyere Cemetery and Memorial, together with the Son Ok Cemetery and Memorial at the head of Zigin Dere (Gully Ravine), in 1947 and 1948 respectively.[5]

The largest and most dramatic Turkish memorial stands on the site of Eskihisarlik Burnu (Old Fortress Head) at Morto Bay, which was designed to rival both the scale and ambition of the Cape Helles Memorial to the Missing, and was begun in 1954. The design resulted from a national competition held in 1944 and the Canakkale Sehitleri Aniti (Turkish Martyrs' Memorial) was partly financed by public subscription. It takes the form of a four-pillared arch standing 41.30m high and dominates the landscape, being visible far out at sea and from many different points inland. Finished in 1960, the area has been added to ever since and now includes a series of bas-reliefs affixed to the pillars which tell the Turkish narrative of Canakkale. Other memorials and groups of statues, including a symbolic cemetery and a memorial garden, have been added and a modern museum sited below the arch was opened in 1971. In 1973 the peninsula was made a National Park with the title Gelibolu Yarimadasi Tarihi Milli Parki – with a new visitor centre constructed at Kabatepe and with its headquarters at Eceabat (Maidos).

Between 1960 and 1983 a variety of military governments have resulted from the seizure of power by the military forces in Turkey at perceived moments of constitutional crisis. In 1981 all political parties were suspended in what was known as 'Ataturk Year', the anniversary of Mustafa Kemal's birth. Since the adoption of a new constitution in 1983, democratic government has been normal and Turkey has pursued a line of application for membership of the European Union as the next step from its 1963 Treaty of Association. Much of the remaining Turkish memorialisation at Gallipoli has taken place since those turbulent times, and further memorials and cemeteries were added in the early 1960s, the 1980s and 1990s. For example, the first Martyrs' Memorial at Seddulbahir was erected in 1986 to commemorate those members of the fortress garrison killed during the British and French shelling of 3 November 1914. The 57th Regiment Memorial Park was constructed and dedicated in 1992 at the time of the initiation of economic co-operation between the countries bordering the Black Sea and the opening of the Ataturk Dam in the same year. The 57th Regiment Memorial Park includes a large statue of a Turkish soldier designed to commemorate the bravery and patriotism of those Turkish forces which confronted the landings in April 1915.

In 1989 Turkey had begun the demilitarisation of the Gallipoli area, a process largely completed by the late 1990s. Since demilitarisation, the project of continuing Turkish memorialisation has taken on the spirit of reconciliation, and as the twenty-first century began it was decided to designate the landscape the

Fig. 5 Statue of Mustafa Kemal in 1915 at Gallipoli.

Fig. 6 Turkish Martyrs' Memorial.

Fig. 7 Mustafa Kemal statue surveying Anzac.

Fig. 8 Turkish symbolic cemetery garden of remembrance.

Gallipoli Peninsula Peace Park. At North Beach, a large area was created as the Anzac Commemorative Site and was dedicated on the eighty-fifth anniversary of the landings, in 2000. Annual commemorations are now held on the peninsula to mark the deeds of Australia, New Zealand, Turkey, France and Britain, although the Anzac Day dawn service held at Lone Pine and Chunuk Bair attracts growing numbers of Australians and New Zealanders to the peninsula.[6]

In the face of militant Islam, some in Turkey have argued that Gallipoli should be seen as part of a jihad or holy war between Islam and the Christian world. As such, there have been calls to designate the peninsula where the fighting took place as a holy site, although it should be pointed out that followers of Islam fought on both sides in 1915.

The ongoing memorialisation of Gallipoli in the ninety-five years since 1915 not only demonstrates the contested meaning of the prevailing narrative of events in the past, but has also shown how far meanings are adapted to meet contemporary needs in the changing post-war political climate in which the original combatant nations found themselves. Mehmed Fasih, in his diary of the fighting at Lone Pine in 1915, states that on 5 November 1915 some 5,000 rounds and ten grenades had been used in the overnight fighting, but at 5.30 a.m. 'glorious daylight bathes everything … at times for entire minutes, there is no firing. During such fleeting moments, silence establishes perfect harmony with a lovely morning increasingly bathed in sunlight, and one has time to think of the future.' Fasih was appointed Chief of Staff of Land Forces in 1955 before retiring in 1959 after forty-five years' service. He died, aged 70, in 1964, forty-nine years after he had survived the fighting at Lone Pine. His life spanned the same period as that of the new Republic of Turkey, for whom the memorialisation of their first victory remains alive with meaning.

Notes

1 Commonwealth War Graves Commission Information Sheet, 'The Gallipoli Campaign 1915'.
2 N. Steel, *Gallipoli* (Barnsley: Battleground Europe Leo Cooper, 1999).
3 T.J. Pemberton, *Gallipoli Today* (London: Ernest Benn Ltd, 1928).
4 A. Mango, *Ataturk* (London: John Murray, 1999).
5 R. Kasaba (ed.), 'Turkey in the Modern World', *The Cambridge History of Turkey*, Vol. 4 (Cambridge: Cambridge University Press, 2008).
6 H.B. Danisman (ed.), *Lone Pine (Bloody Ridge) Diary of Lt Mehmed Fasih* (Istanbul: Diezler Kitabar, 2001).

Three

UNVEILING SLAVERY MEMORIALS IN THE UK

Nikki Spalding

The public recognition of anniversaries offers individuals, families, groups, communities and societies opportunities to celebrate or memorialise significant events in their personal or shared histories. Some anniversaries – in particular the centenaries of major events – take place on a national or sometimes international scale. As such, commemorative years can be viewed as a revealing manifestation of what particular communities (whether real or imagined) choose to remember about their past, and therefore they act as a symbolic expression of contemporary values and identities. For example, this very book has been produced to coincide with the commemoration of ninety years of The Royal British Legion, an organisation which is itself synonymous with remembrance, in particular through its co-ordination of the Poppy Appeal, through which millions of people each year express their support of those who have served and are currently serving in the armed forces.

Sometimes commemorative years are conceived in order to bring previously 'hidden histories' to the attention of the public, through the use of a range of media, including exhibitions, documentaries, television dramas, radio programmes, films, literature, events, public lectures, artwork and memorials. In such cases, the intention is not just to remember a particular aspect of the past, but to provide opportunities for people to increase their awareness and understanding of both the history and its legacies. A great example of this widely accepted correlation between memorialisation and learning occurred in 2007. On 25 March 2007 it had been 200 years since a parliamentary bill was passed to abolish the slave trade in the former British Empire. This historic event was nationally

Fig. 1 'Captured Africans' memorial in Lancaster, by artist Kevin Dalton-Johnson.

commemorated in Britain, with the government tag-line of 'Reflecting on the past, looking to the future', and the Heritage Lottery Fund awarded millions of pounds to projects related to the bicentenary.

There are physical traces of the stories and legacies of transatlantic slavery throughout the British landscape. In fact, if you scratch beneath the surface of many British heritage sites, cities or industries, there are tangible links to the slave trade, for example at the docklands of London or the cotton mills of Manchester. Less obviously connected are the stately homes built by families that made their fortune from the slave trade in the West Indies (e.g. Harewood House in West Yorkshire) or the street made famous by The Beatles that is in fact named after a Liverpool merchant who was a slave ship owner and vocal anti-abolitionist ('Penny Lane', after James Penny). There is also the statue in the centre of Bristol that commemorates the philanthropy of a local merchant and Member of Parliament, who acquired his wealth through the slave trade and was a member of the Royal African Company (Edward Colston, 1636–1721). Perhaps most intriguing is the plaque in St Mary's churchyard that commemorates 'Nottingham's first black entrepreneur', who was brought to England as a slave at 3 years old and who went on to start an employment agency (George Africanus, 1763–1834).

Until recent years, many of the connections between the slave trade and British history had either not yet been articulated by historians or had been hidden, distorted or misrepresented in both the pages of the history textbook and the buildings and sites of the heritage sector. However, the 2007 bicentenary acted as a catalyst in redressing these errors and omissions within public memory. The International Slavery Museum (Liverpool), the Wilberforce House Museum (Hull) and the 'Atlantic Worlds' gallery at the National Maritime Museum (London) each unveiled substantial redevelopments in 2007. These new exhibitions were carefully researched and designed by curatorial teams who worked in consultation with communities, interest groups and specialist historians in order to present a more truthful, thorough, accessible and appropriate representation of the history of slavery.

In addition, a number of memorial projects emerged in anticipation of and in response to this heightened interest in the history of transatlantic slavery. Since at least the 1980s, monuments and memorials have been perceived as potential sites for learning and not just as 'sites of memory'. Consequently, artists and designers are tasked with creating models that have a pedagogical purpose as well as an aesthetic and affective appeal, if they are to be successful in having their designs commissioned. Although there has been a campaign to erect a sculpture in Hyde Park to remember enslaved Africans and their descendants, the £1.5 million needed for the bronze statue has not yet been raised and 'Memorial 2007' has not come to fruition, despite the backing of London's mayor, Boris Johnson. It may be that the sheer scale of a 14ft-high granite and bronze memorial depicting 'six larger than life free-standing figures, each of whom represents a part of the slave

Fig. 2 Map of 'triangular trade' and figures of enslaved Africans at base of 'Captured Africans' memorial.

story', [1] and the highly visible nature of the proposed location in the nation's capital, are key factors in preventing this project from moving forward, whereas smaller memorial projects that are removed from the gaze of international tourists and diplomats have had greater success.

The Slave Trade Arts Memorial Project (STAMP) in Lancaster unveiled its own memorial artwork in 2005, titled 'Captured Africans'. STAMP was formed as a partnership between the city council, the museums service, campaign groups and the county education service. The STAMP team worked with artists, schools and community groups in order to increase public awareness of the link between Lancaster and the shipping of enslaved Africans across the Atlantic. The memorial is roughly the same height as the one proposed for London's Hyde Park, yet this quayside sculpture is less explicitly confrontational; the artist, Kevin Dalton-Johnson, opted for an abstract representation of the history of slavery as opposed to the realism offered by the Memorial 2007 design.

'Captured Africans' takes the shape of a ship (see Fig. 1) that is imbued with words and materials that invoke the slave trade ('wealth', 'cotton', 'rum', 'mahogany', coins encased in acrylic), as well as incorporating a mosaic of the 'triangular trade' (Europe, Africa and the Americas; see Fig. 2) and an inscription that details the names of slave ships with links to Lancaster (see Fig. 3). Perhaps most inspiring of all are the modest depictions of captured Africans that are positioned on top of the mosaic base of the sculpture. These are the product of a series of

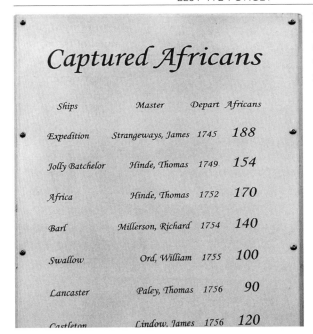

Fig. 3 List of slave ships with links to Lancaster inscribed on the side of the 'Captured Africans' memorial.

workshops, where after discussing the subject matter and studying diagrams of slave ships, a group of young people from Lancaster made these simple figures in clay, with a little assistance from Kevin, before selecting which ones they thought were the best. These were then cast in iron for use in the finished memorial.

Kevin describes himself as a 'pedagogic artist', and when interviewed about the design, he explained that he was mindful of not using stereotypical portrayals of slaves, as 'it could stir up quite large pangs of guilt within the public, who may not want to look at it for that reason, and therefore the sculpture would not meet one of my main objectives, to be informative'.[2] This is why he chose to focus on exhibiting the nature of the slave trade itself, rather than recreating the rhetoric of the popular images of the abolition movement; for example, Josiah Wedgwood's anti-slavery medallion, 'Am I Not a Man and a Brother?' (c. 1787). It is this determination to engage and educate onlookers, to enhance both cognitive and affective understandings of that which it memorialises, coupled with the innovative and thoughtful ways in which the artist worked with local communities, which makes this artwork such a success.

Commemoration is in part an act of unveiling, in both the literal and figurative meanings of the word. However, remembering a 'difficult heritage' such as the history of the transatlantic slave trade and African slavery in the Americas may serve to unveil things about a historic site, museum, city or nation that makes the past 'unsettling' and potentially divisive; a difficult heritage can be defined as 'a past that is recognised as meaningful in the present but that is also contested and awkward for public reconciliation with a positive, self-affirming contemporary identity'.[3] People might feel proud of Britain's historic role in bringing about the abolition of the slave trade, yet simultaneously feel ashamed of the nation's prominence in the trade – particularly during the eighteenth century – and the enormous profits that British companies, industries and plantation-owning families made out of the labour, suffering and deaths of enslaved Africans.

Active remembrance is not just about unveiling new memorials or monuments, or about marking commemorative days, events or years. Before and beyond 2007, slavery remembrance is about ripping off the veil that has been drawn over the history of transatlantic slavery, re-imagining the meaning of British history and heritage, and – perhaps most importantly – giving a voice to the nameless millions of enslaved Africans, the forgotten, the 'disremembered and unaccounted for'.[4]

Notes

1 Memorial 2007, *The Sculpture: the artist's concept* [www.memorial2007.org.uk/the-sculpture].
2 A. Rice, *Art about Slavery* (2009) [www.uclan.ac.uk/schools/journalism_media_communication/].
3 S. Macdonald, *Difficult Heritage* (New York: Routledge, 2009).
4 T. Morrison, *Beloved* (New York: Plume, 1987).

Changing Cultures
of Remembrance

T HE rationale, form and focus of remembrance are constantly changing in contemporary culture. The memorials to the Falklands War piece suggests that a considerable range of public and private motivations exist in the use of memorials. The motivation for acts of remembrance for the Cold War, such as at Greenham Common, where nobody actually lost their lives, might have been considered strange by earlier generations. Others would question the motivation for memorials to animals, and what this says about human sentimentality and the differing views of animal/human relationships over time. However, such memorials have a surprisingly long history. Holocaust Memorial Day, which started as a simple narrative of Nazi persecution of the Jews in the 1930s and 1940s, has now developed into a far wider commemoration of subsequent genocides, so fostering a desire for future prevention.

Four

PUBLIC/PRIVATE COMMEMORATION OF THE FALKLANDS WAR:
Mutually Exclusive or Joint Endeavours?

Karen Burnell & Rachel Jones

Commemoration can occur both publicly and privately, and this is in part to do with the idea that commemoration is the expression of both public and private narratives of war. Narratives convey memories about events. It is thought that public narratives of war may be created through more public or demonstrative acts of commemoration, such as memorialisation, organised commemorative practice, media representation and the public telling of war narratives;[1] whereas private narratives refer more to the individual memories of veterans, which may be shared with only a few people or recalled as a private commemorative act. This chapter introduces the idea that how wars are commemorated can have an impact on the veterans of these wars by either complementing or contradicting the private narratives they have created. It is argued that in the latter half of the twentieth century, the rise of subjectivity and the end of post-war historical certainty has resulted in a change in the nature of memorials and public commemoration. Due to this, more recent conflicts may not be commemorated or perceived by the public with the same 'justness' as the First or Second World Wars; whilst on a personal level, the feelings of modern service personnel may be no different from their World War counterparts.

The Falklands War presents an interesting case study because, whilst being a latter twentieth-century conflict, public narratives of the war reflect Second World War narratives. However, whilst borrowing narratives, Falklands War narratives are not quite as accepted as Second World War narratives, nor are they seen with the same 'fear, shame, guilt, social approval and effective control' as other post-Second World War narratives such as the Gulf War.[2] Such complex public narratives can often make it harder for veterans of conflict to come to terms with their experiences. This chapter uses Rachel Jones' historical research on Falklands War memorials and Karen Burnell's psychological research with Falklands War veterans to explore the relationship between public and private commemoration and the potential impact that both complementary and contradictory narratives have on veteran mental health.

Memorials commemorate by marking an event and supporting memory.[3] As such, memorials can be used to reinforce the publicly accepted narrative by triggering memory. There are a number of Falklands memorials in Hampshire. Here we present two examples and discuss how they support two contrasting narratives of the Falklands War. The Gosport Hard Mosaic Memorial was dedicated by Margaret Thatcher in 1997 on the fifteenth anniversary of the end of the conflict. It is circular in shape, depicting a two-dimensional globe aligning the Falkland Islands geographically with the United Kingdom. The Gosport Hard Mosaic also forms a direct link between the Falklands and D-Day. The two wars are aligned geographically, which encourages the viewer to draw comparisons between the Falklands War by using the Second World War narrative perhaps to legitimise the Falklands War. Whilst there was a massive flurry of commemorative activity when the memorial opened, it is not generally used to commemorate the Falklands War. That is, it is not used as a site of memory; no commemorative objects are left at it and it seems to hold no special meaning for the veterans or their families.

The Sallyport Memorial is in Old Portsmouth, around 200m from Portsmouth cathedral and another memorial plaque. The memorial consists of a large plaque listing the names of those lost, and the inscription reads:

ROYAL NAVY, ROYAL MARINES, ROYAL FLEET AUXILIARY,
MERCHANT NAVY.
THIS MEMORIAL IS DEDICATED TO THE MEMORY OF
THE ROYAL NAVY, THE ROYAL MARINES
THE ROYAL FLEET AUXILIARY AND THE MERCHANT NAVY,
WHOSE NAMES ARE
RECORDED HERE.
THEY GAVE THEIR LIVES IN THE SERVICE OF THIS COUNTRY
AND FOR THE DEFENCE OF FREEDOM, IN
THE FALKLAND ISLANDS AND THE SOUTH ATLANTIC
1982.

Unlike the Gosport Hard Mosaic, the Sallyport plaque is used more, perhaps serving as a site of pilgrimage by veterans and families. Items such as naval insignia, personal notes and photographs are left at the site, with activity peaking around Christmas and the anniversaries of the major events of the war. This memorial may be used more than the Gosport Hard Mosaic as it appears to be more relevant to private narratives of veterans and their families. Importantly, it is not compared in any way with the Second World War, and stands alone as a memorial to the Falklands War. As such, it may be more consistent with the private narratives held by Falklands War veterans and their families, and perhaps also public narratives.

Whilst memorials can trigger and/or support public commemoration, they may also trigger and influence private commemoration. As such, they can impact on how a veteran feels about a war by complementing or contradicting their personal narrative. Personal narratives allow veterans to reflect on the importance of the war to them, their actions, and loss of comrades. Through such reflection a veteran may be better able to come to terms with their experiences.[4] The creation of the private narrative does not occur in isolation. Recent research with Falklands War veterans indicates that resources such as support from society are vital.[5] Veterans may get a sense of the level of societal support by the way a war is depicted in a memorial or through acts of public commemoration. This in turn can help or hinder veterans coming to terms with their memories. For instance, communication with family members can be triggered by public commemoration:

> I think that's [twentieth anniversary] when it sort of really sunk home to both of us that more things need to be talked about ... we did discuss things in greater depth and I think it's helped both of us ... because not only has it helped me to sort of off load things that are on my mind ... it's also given her a greater understanding of what's in my mind.

Without positive support, veterans can be dissuaded from sharing private memories. However, when support is felt from society as a whole this can help veterans to think positively about their actions in war: 'And it [society's reaction] was genuinely good ... and it was good to have ... I think if we'd have come back to ill-feeling ... I think that would have definitely coloured my view about the war ... It would be much different.'

Returning to the two memorials presented earlier, Sallyport is used frequently, whilst Gosport is largely ignored. We argue that this might be because the Gosport Hard Mosaic tries to draw parallels between the Falklands War and the Second World War, which is not an accepted public narrative. Indeed, Falklands veterans also have issues with these comparisons: 'Make no mistake it was a proper war ... people died ... it was a fairly bitter affair ... I don't feel that even after that ... that I did as much as guys in the Second World War.'

Memorials are used to support acts of commemoration, but also to help people interpret and make sense of wars. They do so either by directly drawing comparisons between past and present conflicts, or simply by how a memorial is used during commemoration. Such use creates public narratives. Unlike members of the general public, veterans have personal narratives of war. When public and private commemoration complement one another, this can be hugely beneficial for veterans. However, when public and private commemoration contradict one another, the impact on veterans can be detrimental and can affect a veteran's ability to come to terms with their experiences. The role memorials play in establishing and perpetuating public narratives has implications for the ways in which we as a society memorialise and commemorate war.

Notes

1 D. Thelen (ed.), *Memory and American History* (Bloomington & Indianapolis: Indiana University, 1990).

2 D.A. Welch, 'Remember the Falklands? Lessons of a Misunderstood War', *The International Journal*, 52(3) (1997), pp. 483–507.

3 D. Hayden, *The Power of Place: Urban Landscapes as Public History* (London: MIT Press, 1995).

4 K.J. Burnell, P.G. Coleman & N. Hunt, 'Coping with traumatic memories: Second World War veterans' experiences of social support in relation to the narrative coherence of war memories', *Ageing & Society*, 30(1) (2010), pp. 57–78.

5 K.J. Burnell, N. Hunt & P.G. Coleman, 'Developing a model of narrative analysis to investigate the role of social support in coping with traumatic war memories', *Narrative Inquiry*, 19(1) (2009), pp. 91–105.

Five

MEMORIALS AND INSTRUCTIONAL MONUMENTS:

GREENHAM COMMON & UPPER HEYFORD

Daniel Scharf

This paper will look at how heritage sites can work as memorials and instructional monuments. An examination of the particular cases of the former RAF/USAF bases at Greenham Common and Upper Heyford will describe some of the interventions made by owners, English Heritage and central and local government departments. For some, the Cold War will have remained in the background, whilst for others the threat of nuclear holocaust made a deep impact on their lives. How these two sites are presented and made available to this and future generations will help or hinder the keeping of memories about and commemoration of the Cold War.

The importance of former RAF Greenham Common (about 20 miles south of Oxford) lies in its role during the Cold War, which 'for many ... represented a fearsome epoch in modern history'[1] – although the cashing in of the peace dividend has resulted in a level of landscape change which now severely limits the opportunities for different audiences to explore their individual and collective pasts.

Greenham Common was the site chosen for storing ninety-six ground-launched cruise missiles from 1981 to 1992 (sixty-three being stationed at RAF Molesworth), to fill what was perceived by some to be a missile gap between NATO and the USSR/Warsaw Pact, accompanied by the Greenham Women's peace camp(s), which were located at the base for all of that period. When the site was declared surplus to 'defence' requirements a proposal to make the missile silos part of a heritage site was rejected by Newbury District Council. The former military buildings were transferred to the Greenham Common Trust,

Fig. 1 Baby clothes and pictures hang beneath anti-nuclear signs on the fence surrounding the US air force base at Greenham Common.

Fig. 2 The crossing of the runways at Greenham.

which was created for that purpose, and the District Council took over the former airfield. Whilst the aggregate from the runways has been recycled into local building projects, the crossing of the main runway has been preserved (see Fig. 2) as a token memorial.

The disarming of the Ground Launched Cruise Missile Alert and Maintenance Area (GAMA) site was one result of the Intermediate-Range Nuclear Forces Treaty signed by Presidents Reagan and Gorbachev in 1987, and the missile bunkers were made scheduled monuments in 2002.[2] The opportunity to keep the GAMA site in the ownership of the council or the trust was missed and the site was sold by the Ministry of Defence to a private company intending some kind of storage use. The heritage potential of the cruise missile site has been privatised, made inaccessible to the public and largely obscured from view behind retained security fencing.

The control tower was transferred to the District Council having been identified as being suitable to house a museum, but remains unused and derelict. The Greenham Women secured a small area of land, initially called a Commemorative and Historic Site, where one of the camps had been located close to the entrance of the New Greenham Park, the collection of former military buildings now used for business purposes and a community and arts centre. What has been renamed as the Peace Garden (see Fig. 3) is at some distance and visually removed from both the former airfield and GAMA. The garden is landscaped with gravel, an oak tree, standing stones, a stone fountain and iron sculpture – elements all intended to be symbolic of the non-violent protest by thousands of women. There is also a memorial to the one protester who died close by as a result of a traffic accident.

Documentaries and films have been made of the protest and in the introduction to *Greenham Women; Non-violent women – v – The Crown prerogative*, Sarah Hipperson says that there are 'several books written about the Women's Peace Camp … two relating to the day-to-day lives of women … as part of the continuous witness against the sighting of … Cruise Missiles'.[3] It was the purpose of Hipperson's book to explain how the women tested the legality of nuclear weapons. Whilst no longer sited at Greenham, such weapons remain fundamental parts of our Cold War inheritance and heritage. The Greenham Women were aware of the potential of anniversaries and extended their protest to the Atomic Weapons Research Establishment nearby at Aldermaston (famous for CND marches) on Hiroshima and Nagasaki days, 6 and 9 August. Greenham Common is advertised for visiting on Holocaust Memorial Day, the anniversary of the discovery of Auschwitz by the Russian army on 25 January 1945.

The feats of the women protesting for so long in such harrowing conditions should stand out as a remarkable chapter in our national history. It is disconcerting that there is no museum or coherent interpretation of the landscape at Greenham to help prevent the fading of the memory of both the cruise missiles and the protesters. The preservation of GAMA, the control tower and vestiges

Fig. 3 Greenham Peace Garden: a fitting memorial for the protesters but not saying much about the *raison d'être* of the protest – the threat of genocidal war?

Fig. 4 The NATO runway at Upper Heyford being put to use on Holocaust Memorial Day, 2007, themed 'Imagine … Remember, Reflect, React'.

of the airbase retain the potential for acts of remembrance. Histories of both the use of Greenham by the USAF and the non-violent protest might be picked up from other sources but, in its current state, the potential of the site to stir emotions applicable to the remembrance of these truly momentous events is entirely lacking.

Upper Heyford (about 12 miles north of Oxford) was one of the RAF airfields chosen in 1950 for use by the USAF Strategic Air Command, described by English Heritage as 'hardened in the 1970s and 1980s, including the construction of Hardened Aircraft Shelters … This, the final phase of the Cold War, produced very distinctive military landscapes which will be seen as encapsulating approaches to the defence of the realm',[4] albeit by a foreign power. Since about 2006 English Heritage has regarded Upper Heyford as 'the most complete example of … such a Cold War landscape in Britain'. This stance has not been translated into comprehensive protection by them of even the military areas. For example, only nine of the fifty-six hardened aircraft shelters are scheduled monuments and there is nothing to stop the owners from removing the razor wire from the perimeter fence. English Heritage is hoping that its limited resources will not be called on to help the owners make the heritage asset available to the public. The ambition of the owners (supported by English Heritage) has gone no further than to make a heritage centre and coach tours of the site available on four days each month; the extent to which this level of access does justice to a site of pre-eminent importance, as a survivor of the Cold War, must be questionable.

The USAF returned the site to the MoD in 1994, soon after which a legal option to sell was entered into with a consortium of house builders. The government seemed oblivious to the heritage potential and no safeguards were put in place to limit the scale of the physical changes. An application made in 2010 to have the base included on the tentative list for World Heritage Site status produced very mixed messages from the interested parties. The head of English Heritage thought that some European mark would be more achievable.[5] The ward councillor found it ridiculous to equate the importance of a collection of derelict bunkers to the Great Wall of China or the Statue of Liberty. The council and the owners are undecided about the possible effects of having the undisputed world heritage importance of the site receive official recognition with the consequent glare of publicity and promise of high visitor numbers.

Over the last fifteen years most of the housing and many of the buildings have been let out. Most controversially, runways and hard-standings have been used for car storage, as the jobs created are deemed by the planning authorities in local and central government to outweigh the harm being caused to the historic environment. Individual and group visits have been arranged through the owner's estate office (the site was sold by the MoD in 2006). Visitors have been shown a video about the history of the airfield since 1914 and the improvised tour can include the nuclear bomb stores; the Quick Reaction Alert (QRA), where nine F111s were kept at a high level of readiness in case an attack on the Soviet Bloc was required; the NATO runway, from which such an attack would be launched; and the Battle Command Centre, from where it would have been organised. All the facilities are in the state left by the USAF and not yet prepared for the tourist gaze. The owners have also co-operated with requests for special visits as shown in Fig. 4.

Both sites will continue to be visited by USAF ex-servicemen (and their families) who saw themselves as being on the front line in defence of the free world, and Greenham will remain a place of pilgrimage and mixed memories for the women who gave so much of their lives to the peace protest. As instructional monuments, the relatively unchanged state of the Cold War landscape at Upper Heyford should assist visitors in understanding the history of the Cold War period and for reflecting on the potential of nuclear war, stirring the memories of those who lived through the period and the uncertain threat of annihilation. In contrast, most visitors to Greenham are those walking dogs over the common, not obviously aware of the significance of past events and to whom the sparse Cold War remains are intriguing rather than informative.

Notes

1 English Heritage, *Military Buildings Selection Guide* (English Heritage, March 2007).
2 Ibid., p. 12.
3 S. Hipperson, *Greenham Women* (self-published, 2005), p. 1.
4 S. Thurley, 'Harrowing heritage', *Financial Times* (17 September 2010).
5 'RAF base heritage bid is ridiculous – councillor', *Banbury Guardian* (29 July 2010), p. 11.

Six

WHAT DIFFERENCE CAN A DAY MAKE?

Carly Whyborn

Holocaust Memorial Day, which takes place on 27 January, the date Auschwitz was liberated, may be only one day but its impact is intended to be felt throughout the year. Taking place in the United Kingdom since 2001, and formally adopted by the UN as an international event in 2005, Holocaust Memorial Day is an opportunity for all people, of all ages, in every community to learn the lessons of the past to create a safer, better future. By using the Holocaust and acts of Nazi persecution as the starting point, everyone in the United Kingdom can begin to create a picture of what happens when the differences between people are not respected.

Holocaust Memorial Day looks at how acts of genocide can develop almost without people noticing; it asks everyone to think about the language of hatred, how people can be classed into 'us' and 'them' and, importantly, ensures that people acknowledge how the systematic persecution of those the Nazis deemed to be 'different' culminated in the death of around 11 million men, women and children, including 6 million Jews. Sadly, when the world learned about the full scale of the Nazi atrocities and uttered the words 'never again' this was not a promise it kept. Holocaust Memorial Day seeks to remind everyone that genocides have taken place again and again – in Cambodia in the 1970s, in Bosnia in 1992–95, Rwanda in 1994 and, as the recent atrocities of 2003 onwards attest, the genocide in Darfur.

Whilst Holocaust Memorial Day aspires to raise awareness of these atrocities, it also endeavours to cast a light on the way people live in our communities today. Statistics on those who are discriminated against or who suffer in hate crimes act as a reminder that the world has not truly learnt from the past. So can one day really make any difference? Millions of people are working together to try to ensure that it does.

The number of events held by all kinds of organisations has increased by 65 per cent in the last five years, bringing the total number of events held in the UK to 758 for Holocaust Memorial Day 2010. These events – ranging from small, reflective occasions to large-scale events taking place over a week – show the strength of commitment there is to Holocaust Memorial Day in the UK. With no right or wrong way to mark Holocaust Memorial Day, organisers use their events to commemorate the victims of the Holocaust, Nazi persecution and subsequent genocides and to provide informal education. The intention is to promote community cohesion and encourage everyone to value diversity in cities, towns and villages. Holocaust Memorial Day can prompt the launch of hate-crime prevention initiatives or city-wide awareness, raising pledges so that communities feel the impact of Holocaust Memorial Day not only on 27 January, but throughout the year. History suggests that genocide develops in small stages and begins when people discriminate against others, so Holocaust Memorial Day asks everyone to address the ways they behave and interact with one another, making the lessons of the past relevant to all citizens today.

The Nazi attempt to wipe out European Jewry is at the foundation of Holocaust Memorial Day commemorations. Nazi hatred for Jews knew no bounds; it built on pre-existing anti-Semitism and slowly took away the rights and individuality of all Jews in occupied countries. This gradual process of exclusion led to full-on genocide, culminating in the mass murder of 6 million Jewish men, women and children. Furthermore, anyone who did not fit their narrow idea of what it was to be 'normal' – the Roma and Sinti, homosexuals, the mentally and physically disabled, trade unionists, Freemasons, Jehovah's Witnesses, political opponents, black Europeans and those considered 'asocial' – were persecuted under the Nazi regime. However, as this was not the only regime to commit genocide, Holocaust Memorial Day event organisers also focus on experiences from other genocides, so challenging perceptions of past and present. Viviana Archer-Todde, who organises the Holocaust Memorial Day events in Calderdale, of which there were thirty-nine in 2010, said: 'I realised that people genuinely thought that the Holocaust was the only genocide that has happened and it motivated me further to remind people that hatred still exists in many, many kinds of forms and that's why I became so inclusive when I commemorate Holocaust Memorial Day in Calderdale.'[1]

Holocaust Memorial Day provides everyone with the opportunity to remember the victims of the Holocaust, Nazi persecution and subsequent genocides and to honour the survivors of those atrocities. Holocaust survivors speak at Holocaust Memorial Day events about how the audience can play a role in keeping the memory of the past alive and the impact that remembrance and action can have on communities. The day also empowers ordinary citizens to organise events which fulfil the needs of their community, creating unique, appropriate and powerful events. The events in Halifax ranged from a candle-lit procession to an evening of traditional Bosnian folk music sung by the city's primary schools. For Holocaust Memorial Day 2009, the University of Wales in Cardiff held an awareness-raising event using that year's theme: Stand up to Hatred. This was organised and led by Darfuri asylum seekers and focused on the hatred and discrimination they had faced themselves. For many the Holocaust is central to their events; New Vic Borderlines in Staffordshire worked with young people in the twelve months leading up to Holocaust Memorial Day 2010 to produce a concert, which focused on the Legacy of Hope of Holocaust survivors, drawing different generations together.

People in the UK use Holocaust Memorial Day to remember those whose lives have been wasted in regimes of hatred, and Holocaust Memorial Day Trust guidance is clear that, when reflecting on those murdered, it is essential not to think in terms of statistics but in a way that offers the dignity and respect that each of the victims deserve. However, Holocaust Memorial Day is not simply a case of remembering a series of horrific historical events, but an invitation to learn from the past for the benefit of a shared future. If the promise 'never again' is real then Holocaust Memorial Day must lead to positive action. Holocaust Memorial Day event organisers, such as the Reading Race Council, use the day to launch their annual hate crime prevention strategies in their community, and they ask their audience to renew their commitment to halting hatred, exclusion and discrimination when they see it happening.

Other event organisers use Holocaust Memorial Day, and the free resources produced by the Holocaust Memorial Day Trust, to highlight contemporary issues of racism and discrimination, and ask people to commit to preventing them. On Holocaust Memorial Day 2009, the London Assembly and the Mayor's Office jointly hosted an event where a local victim of disability hate crime spoke about her experiences in London. At the national commemoration of Holocaust Memorial Day 2009, 15-year-old Liam Livermore addressed an audience of faith leaders, dignitaries, government ministers and survivors, stating: 'I would like to see more people being educated on racism and hatred, even if I have to do it myself. I will always stand up to any kind of hatred.' It is the words and actions of tens of thousands of people around the United Kingdom, like Liam, who commemorate Holocaust Memorial Day, which the Holocaust Memorial Day Trust hope will make a change to all communities and to the nation as a whole. Holocaust Memorial Day is therefore also an opportunity for hope, whether in the words of survivors, the stories of rescuers or in the promises made by those attending events; hope is an essential part of Holocaust Memorial Day.

Holocaust Memorial Day is still in its infancy, with Holocaust Memorial Day 2011 marking the eleventh national Holocaust Memorial Day in the UK, but there is evidence that the impact of 27 January is powerful; opening UK newspapers on or around that date shows wide coverage of Holocaust Memorial Day locally and nationally. It is an initiative which aims to do more than remember, but aims to use memories to make a difference today. It is likely to be many more years before the real impact of Holocaust Memorial Day can be seen, heard and felt; however, the early indicators are positive. Whether Holocaust Memorial Day is marked individually or collectively, whether events reach a few people or hundreds, Holocaust Memorial Day offers the chance to strengthen communities, to challenge hatred and discrimination, and to build a future where remembrance of horrors aims to prevent their return. It is only one day in the middle of winter, but the impact of 27 January can resound for the rest of the year.

Notes

1   Holocaust Memorial Day free film, Holocaust Memorial Day 2011 Campaign Pack [http://www.hmd.org.uk/].

Seven

COMMEMORATING ANIMALS: GLORIFYING HUMANS?
REMEMBERING & FORGETTING ANIMALS IN WAR MEMORIALS

Dr Hilda Kean

The 'Animals in War' monument unveiled in London's Park Lane in November 2004 by the Princess Royal was an attempt to incorporate animals explicitly and positively within British history and heritage. It appealed to the notion that the British are 'a nation of animal lovers', but also complemented the fascination with commemoration of the human experience of the Second World War. The memorial attracted wide support from various animal-focused organisations, including Battersea Dogs Home, RSPCA, PDSA and individuals such as Jilly Cooper and Andrew Parker Bowles. It was sculpted by David Backhouse in Portland stone with bronze animal figures, at a cost of £1.4 million.

The monument is in a very public place – the Public Art Advisory Panel of Westminster Council called this a prestigious location – on a traffic island in the middle of a busy thoroughfare with the junction of Upper Brook Street. This does not encourage looking or remembering as it is on a route for cars and buses rather than pedestrians. Unlike many modern war memorials and recent London animal statues, such as that of Hodge, the cat living with Dr Johnson, no animal is named. The animals depicted become representations and generic examples standing in for many others, although many regiments do have named mascots, and stories of named dogs with the troops in Iraq and Afghanistan are widespread.

No human is depicted on the memorial, thus visually animals might seem to be given a privileged and independent status. The overarching sentiment is expressed in a statement which stresses that animals played their part in obtaining

Fig. 1 Frieze at the 'Animals in War' memorial, Park Lane, London.

Fig. 2 Remembrance Day, 2009, 'Animals in War' memorial.

Fig. 3 Frieze at RSPCA clinic, Kilburn, London.

'human freedom'. Furthermore, this is not a memorial to all animals who have died in war, but only to those who 'served and died' alongside 'British and Allied forces'. The controversial statement, distinguishing animals from conscripted humans and civilian victims, 'They had no choice', detracts from questioning of the role of humans in bringing animals into war. The discourse of service and sacrifice dominates and although rituals of remembrance that refer critically to current warfare and animal testing at Porton Down are held annually on Remembrance Sunday, these are not an integral part of the narrative of the memorial. At the moment of recognition of their worth, animals are simultaneously absorbed into a past narrative of worthy sacrifice for the greater – human – good, while their current and continuing plight is being ignored.

Despite the sentiments of some of the press coverage at the time of the Hyde Park memorial's unveiling, this was not the first memorial to commemorate animals in war. The Park Lane sculptural frieze in some ways echoes that still displayed above the entrance to the RSPCA Kilburn branch in London by sculptor Frederick Brook Hitch in the 1930s. Here, not only horses, dogs and elephants, but trench mice were represented as worthy of remembrance. Its setting – unlike other contemporary war memorial friezes – was not in a site of national or local memory, but an 'animal place', on the facade of the local RSPCA clinic. The adjacent plaque again makes a distinction between animals

Fig. 4 'Animals in War' memorial, Australian War Memorial, Canberra.

and humans, suggesting animals 'died for us' in a justified death. It is, how-ever, also stressed that humans need to reciprocate by showing their gratitude through 'kindness and consideration to living animals'.

Less controversially, an Australian 'Animals in War' memorial, unveiled in May 2009 outside the Australian War Memorial in Canberra, commemorates ani-mals who 'performed many essential duties', including those who 'lived with the Australians as mascots or companions', and acknowledges their continuing 'important role in the work of the Australian armed forces'. The memorial con-sists of a bronze horse's head, previously part of an Australian memorial to the Desert Mounted Corps in Port Said in Egypt, destroyed during the Suez Crisis and recreated in Anzac parade.

Artist Steven Mark Holland's original proposal included a 'waterhole' where animals and birds could drink, which would have made the memorial 'a place for all animals',[1] an idea developed in the early twentieth-century memorials to groups of animals in warfare – the horse troughs erected after the Second Boer War. Many thousands of horses had been transported from South America to South Africa to aid the war effort; over 16,000 died on the sea voyage before even reaching the war zone and a further 400,000 animals died during the mil-itary engagement. Horses, and also mules, died mostly from neglect and lack of food and rest, rather than injuries caused in the fighting. The Army Veterinary

Fig. 5 Recreated Desert Mounted Corps memorial, Anzac Parade, Canberra.

Service estimated that only 163 animals died from bullet wounds and a mere three from shellfire. Brigadier Clabby, the veterinary surgeon who wrote the official history of the Royal Army Veterinary Corps declared: 'It has been said that never in the history of any British war has there been such a deliberate sacrifice of animal life and of public money.'[2] Public disquiet led to the erection of memorials. These were not simply representations of horses, and included the trough now filled with flowers in Burstow in Surrey. Initiated by William Tebb, the inscription commemorates 'the mute fidelity of the 400,000 horses killed and wounded ... in a cause of which they knew nothing'.[3] The trough

Fig. 6 Horse trough erected by William Tebb, Burstow, Surrey.

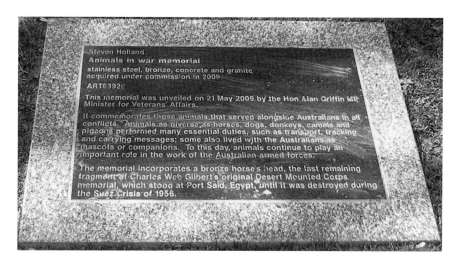

Fig. 7 Plaque at 'Animals in War' memorial, Australian War Memorial, Canberra.

Fig. 8 Close-up of section of frieze, Anzac memorial, Hyde Park, Sydney.

form, albeit on a grander scale, was also incorporated in the 1905 commemoration of where horses had been landed in Port Elizabeth in South Africa. These designs ensured commemorative inclusion in a public space which is still used by horses drinking at the troughs.

Despite the support of former Prime Minister John Howard, insufficient funds were raised to realise Holland's original plans for the Canberra memorial. The accompanying plaque has a less melodramatic text than the London memorial. It 'commemorates those animals that served alongside Australians in all conflicts', and includes those undertaking 'essential duties' and those who 'lived with the Australians as mascots or companions', while recognising that 'To this day, animals continue to play an important role'.[4]

Layers of meaning exist in Holland's work, referring to animal death explicitly and using a statue that had itself been destroyed in warfare to question the destruction of war itself. It also refers to earlier Australian war memorials commemorating the First World War. Joint animal-human commemoration included bas-reliefs by Raynor Hoff on the Anzac memorial in Sydney's Hyde Park, which depicted horses alongside men.

Perhaps the most significant post-First World War memorial to commemorate an animal is the statue by Wallace Anderson to 'Simpson and his donkey', unveiled in 1936 outside the Melbourne Shrine of Remembrance. The story which arose about Jack Simpson Fitzpatrick, a medical orderly from South Shields, and his donkey, who together rescued injured men amidst heavy bombardment in so-called Shrapnel Gully at Gallipoli, contributed to the creation of the Anzac legend, as an 'egalitarian fraternity' of citizen soldiers in the emerging Australian and New Zealand nations.[5] Simpson, though not the donkey, died at Gallipoli in May 1915. Commemoratively, the donkey is usually unnamed and referred

Fig. 9 The first 'man with the donkey' statue, outside the Shrine of Remembrance, Melbourne.

Fig. 10 Simpson and his donkey, reworked outside the Australian War Memorial, Canberra.

to as 'donkey'; in written narratives he is given variously the names of Barney, Murphy and Duffy.[6] The donkey – alongside obvious religious connotations – was seen as an ordinary creature suffering the same fate as his human companion.

Subsequently, different versions of the Simpson myth have been memorial-ised, including a large work outside the Australian War Memorial in Canberra in 1988 by Peter Corlett. The donkey was intended to be 'small yet sturdy and reliable, with a look of reluctant co-operation about him'. While the donkey is key to the artwork, the overall intention of the artist was to produce a work celebrating 'a personal compassion of common humanity'.[7] Whilst it is unlikely Simpson would have been incorporated into a national sense of the past without

Fig. 11 The well-stroked nose of the donkey, Australian War Memorial.

his donkey, the Simpson story – and that of Sandy, the only horse to arrive back in Australia after the campaign in Gallipoli – was promoted to convey patriotic sentiment to future generations. Within these narratives the animal captures the popular imagination – the bronze of Simpson's donkey's nose work is now smooth from being stroked by children – yet the animal is secondary to the idea of 'humanity'.

Memorials which depict the role of animals in warfare recognise the human-animal relationship. They can also implicitly reinforce a hierarchy in which human interests are always put before those of animals. Who, we might ask, are the 'animal' memorials really remembering?

Notes

Thanks to staff at the Australian War Memorial and RSPCA, Canberra.

1   Steven Mark Holland artist's development design, Memorial to Animals in War, RSPCA and Australian War Memorial (AWM archives).

2   J. Clabby, *A History of the Royal Army Veterinary Corps 1919–61* (London: J.A. Allen, 1963), pp. 13–4.

3   As quoted in H. Kean, *Animal Rights. Political and Social Change in Britain* (London: Reaktion Books, 2000), pp. 166–7.

4   Email correspondence from Canberra RSPCA to author, October 2010.

5   S. Macintyre, *A Concise History of Australia* (Cambridge: Cambridge University Press, 1999), pp. 157–9.

6   P. Cochrane, *Simpson and the Donkey: the making of a legend* (Victoria: Melbourne University Press, 1992), pp. 51–5.

7   P. Corlett, 'Simpson and his donkey: a proposal', November 1986, File 89/1234, Australian War Memorial.

Remembrance in Popular Culture

The impact of various forms of commemorative activity in contemporary culture appears to be on the increase. This section thus includes an exploration of some of the recent popular expressions of remembrance, including the spontaneous mass outpouring of sentiment after the Hillsborough Disaster in 1989 and at Princess Diana's death in 1997. Also included is a discussion of various manifestations of remembrance on the internet. Some would argue that a particular nadir was reached in the commercially motivated mass sentimentality seen after Jade Goody's death, where magazines abandoned much that was previously perceived as being of 'good taste' and the restraint offered in formal public cultures of remembrance was almost entirely lacking.

Eight

BENEATH THE MOURNING VEIL:

Mass Observation & the Death of Diana

James Thomas (introduced by Dorothy Sheridan)

September 1997: the tragic news of Princess Diana's death was announced in the media. Almost at once, a trickle and then a flood of letters and reports arrived at the Mass Observation (MO) Archive in the University of Sussex. The letters were written spontaneously (and then later in response to an MO directive or questionnaire) by people who had been contributing over many years to the contemporary phase of MO's documentation of everyday life.

The most substantial study of the resulting collection has been made by James Thomas, formerly a research associate at the Cardiff School of Media, Journalism and Cultural Studies. The extracts below are taken from a paper he wrote in 2002 for the MO Occasional Paper series entitled 'Beneath the Mourning Veil: Mass Observation and the Death of Princess Diana'. He went on to publish his acclaimed and controversial book, *Diana's Mourning: a People's History* (University of Wales Press), later in 2002. Sadly, James himself died very suddenly at the age of 35 in 2007. He had already been in discussion with us at the archive about further research on public grief and expressions of bereavement.

I felt that the MO material should be represented by James rather than by me in this volume and am grateful to Mr and Mrs Thomas for granting permission to reproduce the extracts below. The numbers in square brackets refer to the Mass Observers' numbers which are used to protect their anonymity.

The 'homogenous myth' of Diana's mourning was, of course, of a nation 'united in grief' over the death of their 'People's Princess'. Such an unambiguous meta-narrative of popular reactions was first provided by Tony Blair on the day of

Fig. 1 Do-it-yourself memorial to Diana Princess of Wales, portrayed in the press alongside the announcement that Elton John will sing the rewritten version of *Candle in the Wind* at her funeral, 1997.

the news, in a tribute scripted by Alastair Campbell and borrowed from an old phrase of Julie Burchill's. While the media claimed to detect overwhelmingly positive attitudes to a woman, MO correspondents, by contrast, offered a huge complexity and diversity of opinion. Adulation, praise and qualified identification competed with indifference, equivocation and hostility, sometimes among the same accounts. One of the most common positive sentiments was of a woman who 'had the common touch' [H276], who was 'natural with people and not distanced from them' like the royal family [A2801], and who 'touched hearts with her kindness, her compassion, her mixing with just ordinary people in everyday life' [B736]. As one correspondent, a 35-year-old woman mourner from Manchester, put it: 'In the end Diana was a "people" person – if protocol got in the way she just went around it. To the traditional Royals that must be like trying to stop breathing. Perhaps that is why our grief is so intense – she really was <u>our</u> princess' [B2638].

Contrary to the idea that the mourning saw a collapse of social hierarchies, the elite position Diana embodied often remained present, blocking or qualifying identification. Indeed, even the very depiction of her as 'one of us' illustrated this as it made sense only when based on awareness that she was really 'one of them'. Only because Diana was a member of the elite was her ordinariness worthy of comment. A female civil servant was attending a TUC rally on the Sunday morning and was unaware of the news. She overheard one of the organisers talking about whether the event would go ahead: 'I thought perhaps a famous revolutionary had died … It surprised me to find that trade union activists expressed genuine grief over the death of someone from the aristocracy … It seems absurd to call a woman brought up in wealth and privilege the people's princess' [G2089].

Yet while there were polarities of attitudes on display, such competing assessments were not always mutually exclusive. Individual accounts often conveyed a complex and contradictory mixture of the positive and negative, about her charity work, personality and relationship with the royal family and the press. And while many defined themselves in opposition to Diana's canonisation, which they imagined mourners to be doing, among mourners she was largely seen as a more flawed character who was 'more sinned against than sinning' [B1386]. One observer wrote how 'everything was double-edged with Diana' [F1373] and this was certainly true of the verdicts that followed. Such findings, while at variance with the evidence from media coverage, show close similarities with previous studies of British attitudes to royalty: 'She was as near to an anarchist as you can get in the Royal Family. I always dreamed of what would happen if a Royal became an anarchist and said "up yours" to their ways. Diana did that, almost, well, as best she could' [B2810].

In agreement with such sentiments – but from a negative perspective – were royalists who could not grieve a woman who 'wanted to cause irrevocable damage to our beloved and much needed Royal Family' [D1602]. Some even thought her death had 'happened for the best', as 'we now have one royal family, not two' [J1481]. Inversely, in the accounts of some republicans Diana's antiestablishment status was notable not simply by its total absence, but by the automatic assumption of the opposite perspective towards 'an aristocrat who voted for Thatcher' [P1730], a conservative figure who still symbolised an institution that was 'unarguably, indisputably, fundamentally wrong' [C2722]. Again, however, this is to simplify often complex attitudes. One royalist, for instance, balanced admiration for 'a good person … doing a lot to help various sectors of society' with a defence of the 'perfectly correct' behaviour of the mourning royals once again misrepresented by a vicious press [P1637]. On the other side, a republican man, largely hostile to 'a woman who spent a fortune on clothes and cosmetics', was also captivated by the popular radicalism generated by Earl Spencer's anti-royalist funeral speech [L2393]. In such ways the ambiguity of Diana's life and death, the source of her extraordinary range of appeal, was also the source of its limitations.

It is abundantly clear that [the Mass Observers] were very far from being 'united in grief'. On the contrary, opinions were both divided and polarised across a range of themes, but were also composed of complex, contradictory and ambivalent responses. While existing literature has juxtaposed the responses of 'mourners' against 'dissenters', this reveals a complex popular reaction which was sometimes neither or both. There is, of course, no unproblematic window to popular opinion – despite the habit of opinion polls and the media in presenting themselves as such – and the issue of what is representative is in part a relative one. The depth, sophistication and diversity of Mass Observation evidence certainly compare favourably with overwhelmingly one-dimensional media reporting. This is true collectively but also applies to the measured balance of individual accounts, which were often given further depth as friends, colleagues and families were given space to compete with and often contradict the writer.

Ultimately, analyses of popular opinion deal in the balance of probabilities. In this case it seems highly plausible that Diana's complex life and death should have produced such contrasting responses from a heterogeneous public, composed of distinct and contradictory individual and collective identities – to say nothing of the range of views that the extraordinary events of the mourning stimulated. What is perhaps surprising is not that the country was divided in grief, but the widespread assumption of the reverse perspective. This was captured by one woman, who was 'glad' of the opportunity to write to the archive after a week which had left her 'quite concerned' by a reaction that had left her feeling 'quite isolated' and 'completely out of step with the majority' [T2003]. For others, loyalty to the archive or their strong feelings towards or against the mourning meant that they had already written before receiving the directive. In many ways, of course, the act of writing cannot be separated from what people wrote. For some its production was an active part of mourning, as they supplemented their accounts with poems, decorative stamps or details of written or pictorial tributes that they had offered. One woman finished her account: 'Whoever reads this, I want you to know that I am crying for her now, but that it is one of the greatest honours I have had to be able to write for history here' [B1120]. For sceptics, their contribution could be an active form of resistance and empowerment in the face of the hegemonic mood. One observer announced that he was writing instead of watching a funeral which had 'nothing whatever to do' with him [B2785], while another prefaced her contribution with the expressed determination 'to set the following on record so that the future doesn't think everyone in Britain was round the bloody twist' [P1730]. MO, perhaps uniquely in September 1997, emerges as both a mourning and non-mourning site, providing a forum for the passions of both sides while also catering for those caught somewhere in the middle.

James Thomas' book, *Diana's Mourning: a People's History*, went on to provide a fuller examination of public reactions to the death of Diana and combines the use of Mass Observation with research on the media coverage and on other contemporary sources. Thomas concludes that the media played a significant role not only in reflecting a one-sided reaction to the tragedy, but in constructing this notion; for example, by concentrating their images and interviews on those people who expressed their grief publicly. He wrote:

> It seems highly likely that the myth of a British nation in widespread, emotional, adulatory grief will remain dominant, in negative and positive forms, in popular memory. For the media myth is not only stronger than the unmediated reality of popular experience, but *is* the widely accepted reality, for good or bad of 'the people's' response. That this is the case is a striking illustration not of a democratic week of people power but a dangerously undemocratic week of media power.

It is unlikely now, over a decade later, that we can disaggregate the 'media myth' from 'popular experience', but it would be fruitful to continue James Thomas' work, perhaps using the Mass Observers, to explore the impact of that documentation of public grief. Like the 'myth of the Blitz', it has come to have its own reality in popular memory and may have altered fundamentally the ways in which we view and carry out the social practices of both public and private mourning.

The following sources were consulted in this article:

D. Sheridan, B.V. Street & D. Bloome, *Writing Ourselves: Mass Observation and Literacy Practices* (NJ: Hampton Press, Creskill, 2000).

J. Thomas, *Diana's Mourning: a People's History* (Cardiff: UWP, 2002).

J. Thomas, 'Beneath the Mourning Veil: Mass Observation and the Death of Diana', Mass Observation Occasional Paper No 12 (Brighton: Mass Observation Archive, University of Sussex, 2002).

More information about MO can be found at www.massobs.org.uk.

Nine

REMEMBRANCE IN SPORT:
A Case Study of Hillsborough

Dr Jamie Cleland

In many ways the Hillsborough Disaster was a watershed moment for English football. During the 1980s English football was marred with outbreaks of hooliganism, resulting in a series of measures to protect opposing fans and players from violence. The most notable of these was the introduction of perimeter fencing to stop fans from entering the field of play and attacking rival players or fans. How ironic, then, that the Hillsborough Disaster on 15 April 1989, which was scheduled to be an FA Cup semi-final between Liverpool and Nottingham Forest, was a disaster entirely lacking in any hooligan element. This short essay remembers the day itself, where ninety-six Liverpool supporters eventually died and hundreds were injured as a result of crowd crushing, the immediate aftermath, including the creation of temporary and permanent memorials, and its lasting effect on English football.

Due to its capacity, Hillsborough, the home of Sheffield Wednesday Football Club, was often used as a neutral venue for FA Cup semi-finals during the 1980s. Just before this particular semi-final was about to kick off, thousands of Liverpool fans (some of whom were without tickets) had congregated outside the Leppings Lane end of Hillsborough, which had five pens to hold standing supporters on its lower level. With kick-off approaching, and faced with a large bottleneck of agitated supporters, a decision was made by the South Yorkshire police to open a gate (Gate C) and alleviate what they feared was crushing outside the stadium. This allowed supporters to rush inside, most of whom headed through a narrow tunnel for the two central pens which were already overcrowded. The sheer presence of an increasing number of supporters in an area

Fig. 1 The unfolding disaster at the Hillsborough stadium. *Press Association*

Fig. 2 Flowers on the pitch construct a temporary memorial at Anfield to the Hillsborough Disaster. *Press Association*

Fig. 3 Permanent memorial at Anfield: the Hillsborough memorial preceding the fifteenth anniversary of the incident. *Press Association*

already full unsurprisingly began to crush those at the front against the perimeter fencing and crush barriers.

Watching CCTV footage of the tragedy unfolding in his control room, the commanding officer of South Yorkshire police, faced with the poor reputation of Liverpool fans and the fears of hooliganism at the time, fatally delayed the decision to open the gates surrounding the pitch. When the match began, only six minutes of play was possible before the referee, Ray Lewis, on the advice of a policeman who ran on to the pitch, halted play and the players immediately left the field. Only at this time did the senior police officers realise the extent of the tragedy and ordered the perimeter gates surrounding the pitch to be opened. By this time, however, the sheer force of the supporters pressing against the perimeter fencing had caused it to break and immediately fans started to enter the pitch. Nothing it seemed had prepared the emergency services for this type of unfolding disaster and they were completely overwhelmed. For example, despite a number of ambulances deployed to help those that were injured, only one ever made it on to the playing area.

The immediate aftermath of the disaster was one of grief, both in the United Kingdom and across the world. Almost overnight, temporary memorials were established at both Hillsborough and Anfield, the home of Liverpool Football Club. Indeed, Anfield was immediately opened to the public to pay their respects and it quickly became a shrine of remembrance to those who had died or had been injured. This was most notably symbolised by the goal area immediately in front of 'The Kop' becoming a temporary sea of floral tributes from supporters of clubs from all over the world, as football allegiances were put to one side. This level of mourning lasted for weeks as the city of Liverpool, the club and the game in general struggled to find the spirit to be able to carry on. Every funeral that took place in the weeks after the disaster was attended by a selection of club officials and players, as the club looked to remember those supporters who had helped it become so successful over the years.

Since this time, and helped by the support groups which were established after the disaster, there has been a shift from temporary memorials to more permanent ones to remember those who died. Flames were added either side of the club crest of Liverpool and there have also been permanent memorials erected across both Sheffield and Liverpool. These include a memorial outside Hillsborough, as well as beside the Shankly Gates at Anfield, where each of the ninety-six victims' names is engraved. Other permanent memorials include a stone outside the Anglican cathedral in Liverpool and a headstone at the junction of Middlewood Road, Leppings Lane and Wadsley Lane, close to Hillsborough. At a more local level, some areas of Liverpool have also paid tributes to residents who died with, for example, gardens of remembrance. The anniversary of Hillsborough is also remembered every year across football in general, with a minute's silence held at matches and special ceremonies in Liverpool dedicated to the tenth and twentieth anniversaries of the disaster.

Unsurprisingly, the reaction of the conservative government at the time was to set up a full independent inquiry led by Lord Justice Taylor. The inquiry sat for thirty-one days and published an interim report focusing on the events of the day itself and a final report that made a series of general recommendations on football ground safety. Lord Taylor's interim report stated that the main cause of the disaster was the failure of senior police officers to control the crowd, in particular allowing fans to enter the two central pens once Gate C had been opened. Despite his initial report also blaming Sheffield Wednesday Football Club for their three-year failure to ensure crush barriers met official safety standards (the total capacity of the two pens should have been 1,600, but once the gates were opened it was estimated to contain more than 3,000), an inquest into the deaths returned a majority verdict of accidental death. Groups fighting for justice have been established challenging this, but as of yet no criminal convictions have resulted from this disaster.

So what impact did the final Taylor Report have on football after Hillsborough? Its consequences were profound and the pace at which they occurred was staggering. Perimeter fencing was immediately removed as Taylor focused on major structural changes within English football. At the time of his report the world of football had witnessed a very successful World Cup in Italy, which showcased highly effective modernised stadiums. In comparison, English football had become synonymous with dilapidated stadiums and Taylor sought to change this through the introduction of all-seater stadiums in the top two divisions of

English football and the Scottish Premier Division before the 1994–95 season. Here, clubs were faced with a decision: do they build on and modernise their existing stadium or do they move to a more purpose-built one? Without the Taylor Report it is highly likely that, with the exception of a few notable clubs, many of the proposed changes would not have been made. With grants of only £2 million available, and the costs estimated to be nearer £10 million, many clubs went against Taylor's recommendation and increased ticket prices to generate extra revenue. Thus, whilst capacity originally went down, revenue went up as fans were charged more to sit rather than stand.

The Taylor Report also put the wheels in motion for the level of investment that has been witnessed in football since the disaster. A new Premier League was formed in 1992 and the introduction of satellite television (most notably Sky) has transformed football clubs' revenues. The subsequent development of the Premier League into a global brand as a result of this relationship (both in terms of the finance it generates but also the quality of its football) has also encouraged a large number of wealthy overseas individuals to invest in clubs and this shows no signs of abating.

In summary, from 1992 onwards British football (most notably English) has been transformed. Yet the speed in which this has occurred would not have happened without the Hillsborough Disaster. Hillsborough marked a turning point in the survival of British football and this is possibly the most significant form of remembrance paid to those who lost their lives. Largely unrestricted crowds being crammed into dilapidated stadiums became a thing of the past as football clubs, football supporters and the relevant organisations slowly realised that change was needed. It just took Britain's worst stadium disaster to start the process off.

Ten

BETWEEN EPHEMERA AND POSTERITY:
The Commemorative Magazine Issue

Dr Fan Carter

This chapter sets out to explore the ways in which popular magazines increasingly mark the death of celebrities with special commemorative issues. Commemorative magazines have typically taken two forms: the standalone publication – glossy affairs often sold as part-works – and special issues of established consumer titles. Both make an appeal to posterity, inviting consumers to collect and 'cherish' them, while recognising the transient appeal of both magazines in general and contemporary celebrity culture with its built-in obsolescence.[1] Indeed, such special issues have a habit of reappearing on a regular basis to mark various anniversaries, especially in the case of those featuring Hollywood stars or Princess Diana. Examining these magazines reveals not only the efforts of commercial culture to extend the memorial industry to the ephemeral world of magazines, but also illuminates the particular visual formats and narrative codes through which the commercial commemoration is evinced. I argue that the celebrity image, so central to the success of this magazine format in general, takes on a particular resonance here as a focus for the complex process of remembrance framed by the magazine.

With an issue date of less than a week before she died, the black-framed 'official tribute' edition of *Ok! Magazine* (24 March 2009) was sure to boost sales and court controversy in its efforts to capitalise on Jade Goody's imminent death. The magazine was subject to a barrage of criticism from other more lofty publications and media sources, accused of the worst commercial exploitation with its unseemly hurriedness to commemorate the moment. Such censure was also levied against Goody herself as she struck exclusive deals with the Northern &

Fig. 1 Well-wishers await Jade Goody's cortège before her funeral near St John's Baptist church in Buckhurst Hill. *Press Association*

Shell and Living TV to document her final months. For many, her decision to publicly display the realities of dying exposed the most uncomfortable facets of contemporary celebrity culture with its prurient fascination with the private lives of well-known figures.

While the celebrity magazine might appear a relatively new phenomenon, its antecedents reach back to the nineteenth century and the combination of burgeoning consumer capitalism, (relatively) cheap mechanical reproduction technologies and the development of new markers of popularity and renown.[2] Central to the operations of celebrity culture then, as now, was the ready circulation of the celebrity image around which ideas of both distinction and accessibility played. Significant in this development was the *carte de visite*, a small card-backed photographic portrait that could be collected in albums, displayed in the home, exchanged and gossiped over between friends. These were not only popular with private individuals and used to record the likeness of families and

Fig. 2 A tribute to Jade
Goody using print
media images, at her
funeral at St John's
Baptist church, Essex.
Press Association

friends, but also, and significantly, as a means of displaying royalty and celebrity
figures of the time. Plunkett notes that the publication of the *Royal Album*, comprising a collection of fourteen photographs of the royal family by Mayall in
1860, had reached sales of over 3 million by 1862 alone.[3] He goes on to note that
such mass-produced and circulated images helped to forge a new and very specific affective relationship between the private viewer and the pictured, public
figure. This was marked out by the particular impression of authenticity that
was attached to the new regimes of photographic reproduction, inviting specific
practices of looking in which the arresting verisimilitude fostered an imaginary
intimacy between the viewer and the sitter at a visual level.

Today's spread of celebrity magazines are still distinguished by the central-
ity of the image. Commonly, and despite the distinctions of market and title,
they luxuriate in an excess of photographs of their celebrity subjects captured
in both official set pieces and unofficial candid shots. This is no less true of the

tribute edition which draws together a wealth of visual imagery to picture the individual's life. These are taken from a variety of sources, often including private, domestic images, which rub frames with professional photo shoots and marketing shots. Indeed, this juxtaposition of different, captured moments imitates the structure of the family album and with it the anticipated rituals of viewing and reviewing, sharing stories and memories which make up the private practices of mourning. Here, though, these become public, drawing readers into what Benedict Anderson refers to as an 'imagined community',[4] sharing the practice of remembrance. Significantly, these invitations are often framed by the magazine's history itself as past features and photo shoots are revived through the lens of remembrance.

The commemorative magazine operates within the particular narrative conventions of the eulogy. Life stories are organised in terms of highlights and high points, former scandals re-framed as minor indiscretions, and in their place the enduring quest for personal happiness and fulfilment is emphasised on every page. Irreverent gossip and *Schadenfreude*, the regular motifs of titles such as *Closer* and *Heat*, have no place within these pages. Instead, the celebrity tribute edition models for its readers a sense of the good life, one that has been shaped by affective human relationships and familial bonds. Despite this appeal to universal human values, this good life remains emphatically consumerist, performed in the leisure-scapes of high days and holidays, rather than the more prosaic moments of everyday life. The positive human qualities of the remembered celebrity are extolled in the editorial which proclaims their 'bubbly personalities', 'special gifts' and 'winning smile'. Editorial features assess the legacy of the individual, insisting that they have 'made a difference' in some way. These appraisals point to the broader narrative significance of such celebrity stories; a 'good' life is valued and leaves an enduring mark. These tributes are echoed in the voices of celebrity friends and associates, accompanied by their own smiling photos. In such a way the editorial helps to foster a sense of a tight-knit celebrity community, the 'powerless elite' to which the sociologist Alberoni refers in his critique of the role of stars in society.[5] The sentiments of this exclusive group might resonate with the reader's own, helping to extend a sense of imagined belonging and 'connected knowingness' that many magazine readers feel when reading about the lives of privileged others.[6]

The celebrity tribute magazine is often dismissed as an example of an exploitative remembrance industry which seeks to evoke and then capitalise on what might otherwise remain private feelings of loss. With this comes a disdain for those who profess an affective bond with the constructed figures of celebrity and also the suspicion that such emotions are in some way manufactured; manipulated by the very titles that go on to profit by them.[7] Celebrity magazines do indeed tread a tightrope walk between commerce and commemoration. However, to dismiss them and their readers is perhaps to overlook the ways in which these products of commercial culture are increasingly the sites where our shared cultural memories are formed and re-told. Contemporary celebrity culture also offers a space in which to explore the tensions between public and private images, lives and even deaths.

Notes

1   See S. Holmes & S. Redmond (eds), *Framing Celebrity: New Directions in Celebrity Culture* (London: Routledge, 2006).

2   Ibid.

3   J. Plunkett, 'Celebrity and Community: the Poetics of the *Carte-de visite*', *The Journal of Victorian Culture*, Vol. 8 No 1 (2003), pp. 55–79.

4   B. Anderson, *Imagined Communities: reflections on the origin and spread of Nationalism* (London: Verso, 1991).

5   F. Alberoni, 'The powerless "elite": Theory and Sociological Research on the Phenomenon of the Stars', in S. Redmond & S. Holmes (eds), *Stardom and Celebrity: A Reader* (London: Sage, 2007).

6   See J. Hermes, *Reading Women's Magazines* (Cambridge: Polity, 1995).

7   Such sentiments were expressed in several broadsheets following the deaths of Diana, Princess of Wales, and more recently Jade Goody.

Eleven

WEB-REMEMBRANCE IN A CONFESSIONAL MEDIA CULTURE

Dr Maggie Andrews

In the twentieth and twenty-first centuries, conflict and remembrance have been experienced both at a personal level and through a range of media. From the *Daily Sketch*'s reproduction of images of loved ones picked from battlefields in 1916 to contemporary websites such as YouTube, media has served as an interface between the personal, domestic, unofficial sides of remembrance and its national, official and public role. Whilst arguably, conventional, public remembrance events and commemorative spaces are perceived as using language, imagery and iconography that is institutionally organised, formal, military, structured and emotionally restrained; contemporary forms of web-remembrance have the potential to offer more diverse, even democratic, domestic, emotionally unrestrained forms of remembrance. This publicising of the private face of remembrance may be seen as removed from government, the military and most importantly support for war. It is this, alongside familiarity and informality, which enables web-remembrance to speak to constituencies who may feel excluded from public remembrance in its more traditional forms.

The contemporary internet, the second generation of web-based material – known as Web 2.0 – has four key characteristics: interactivity, user participation, dynamic content and freedom. The material on websites is constantly changing, free from many of the economic or legal pressures that regulate most media content. Whereas traditional media relied upon the consumption of material produced by media organisations, Web 2.0 content emphasises private individuals' input as they upload and download images, videos, music, contacts and content – contributing to, for example, discussion boards or social networking sites. In the last ten years Web 2.0 has given previously hidden and frequently emotionally unrestrained private voices a public space for remembrance. This is congruent with broader cultural shifts in contemporary, media-saturated society, whereby the confessional and therapeutic culture of daytime television, tabloid newspapers, *Ok! Magazine*, Facebook, blogs and Twitter, celebrate intimate revelations and the public airing of what would once have been private emotions and experiences. Such public outpouring of emotions are made possible by significant techno-logical developments, including the miniaturisation, transportability and mass production of new media technology which have enabled the ordinary citizen, armed with only a mobile phone, digital camera and access to the internet, to become both a producer and a consumer of media remembrance texts.

With the USA leading the way, the number of commercial organisations and charities which enable people to produce online global memorials to friends, family, celebrities and even pets who have died is expanding. The freedom to create memorials to articulate loss often takes place within tight aesthetic con-straints, utilising a range of stock images and established iconography: teddy bears, flowers, poppies, candles, angels, alongside private photographs. However, attempts to preserve notions of 'good taste' are often compromised by commer-cial imperatives. Some sites are overtly commercial, charging to set up memorials, to add virtual flowers or carrying a range of adverts for books, country cottages, undertakers and even loans. Access to web memorials may be open or password protected. On www.gonetoosoon.org, for example, visitors are invited to add comments, leave gifts and light candles, join discussion threads and create their own garden of remembrance from a range of memorials. Disregarding con-straints of time and space, such websites enable diffuse networks of families and friends from geographically disparate communities to construct a cyber com-munity of grief.

Anonymity and problems censoring the internet give it a freedom and provide a voice to those whose grief is otherwise hidden, particularly if their emotions and relationships are deemed 'unacceptable' or marginalised. The numerous discussion strands, blogs and dedicated sites for the grieving can facilitate remem-brance and a public outpouring of emotion that would otherwise have no public space. One married woman whose lover had died explained:

> What they gave me was a validation of my relationship with [lover's names] and also a place to share all the emotions that couldn't be expressed due to the secrecy that I maintained to try to save my own husband's face. For me it was the one safe place I had – and the same also went for many of the other people on the site [RW 10-09-09].

Providing a safe place for the 38,000 people who wanted to visit the Facebook memorial page for the gunman Raoul Moat, who evaded police capture for a week in summer 2010, caused controversy and discussion in Parliament. Arguably, the memorialisation of Moat suggested unpalatable but usually hidden discontent and misery within contemporary culture, accompanied by antagonism towards the police and a celebration of lawlessness.

A far more politically acceptable idealisation of the dead is articulated in sites which focus on military personnel; for example, the USA-based www.grief.org has developed an area entitled 'Fallen Heroes'. Here, web memorials provide scope for friends and relations to create an emotionally unrestrained and informal web-remembrance site, which often includes photographs of the bereaved with their parents, siblings, children or partners. Therefore, strongly personal and more confessional domestic forms of remembrance may be created, where families are emphasised as victims of war, tapping into a familiar trope identifiable in news coverage of armed conflicts and in the recent introduction of the Elizabeth Cross.

Arguably, the social networking sites such as Facebook and the bricolage of public and private imagery in the home-made remembrance-themed pop videos on YouTube specifically address contemporary media-savvy youth. In a culture where lives are recorded in, and even acted out for, a range of media, both the Iraq and Afghanistan conflicts were new media wars. They were experienced not only through digital television, but also via combatants' blogs on sites such as www.liveleak.com, and images from the mobile phones or digital cameras of service personnel have provided a bank of images which are later drawn upon by bereaved families and friends to produce Facebook sites and YouTube videos. However, sometimes the style and imagery of traditional remembrance is again utilised or reworked, for example the 'Roll of Honour' may be a structuring theme, albeit visually illustrated and set to a contemporary musical track. Many of the videos are edited with a post-modern borrowing of familiar iconography to blend together clips from national news, images from newspapers, family photographs and informal or personal content. The visual style may borrow from holiday photos with groups of soldiers in Iraq or Afghanistan posing on tanks or raising glasses to the camera, emphasising the previous vitality and life of those recently killed in war. Written commentary frequently attempts to anchor the meaning of visual imagery and maximise emotional impact.

Commercial imperatives of sites such as YouTube again challenge ideas of 'good taste'. Remembrance videos for those killed in Iraq and Afghanistan may be partially obscured by banners advertising a bizarre range of products, from 'Land Rover Cars', 'Looking for Love' or 'Talking Muslim Dolls', to 'Desert Operations, a Computer Game' or pen pals in the forces. Nevertheless, the dynamic content, informal and interactive nature of YouTube and other social networking sites encourages dialogue and ethical debates when comments are added by viewers. These often articulate an increasingly familiar theme of honouring the dead whilst criticising the government's military involvement in Iraq or Afghanistan. For example: 'I FUCKING HATE BRITISH GOVERMENT – Our troops on other hand … i respect them just as my as i respect my own mother' (spelling and punctuation unchanged from dialogue under 'British Army Our Fallen Heroes', YouTube 15/9/2009).[1]

This discursively constructs 'soldiers as victims', as do some of the musical tracks chosen; for example, Kate Bush's 1980s song, *Army Dreamers*, which focuses on the naivety of young boys who wander dreamlike to their death in warfare. The unfettered freedom of the internet also enables a range of much more aggressively articulated debates about governmental decisions, the conduct of the military, recruitment to the armed forces, the militarisation of society, imperialism, religious and national cultural identity. This has caused the scope for discussion on some remembrance videos on YouTube to be disabled, apparently due to 'spiteful and vindictive arguments' undermining the web's customary freedom. The democratic potential of such spaces, which create ethical debate not just within countries but across national boundaries, is missed by the explaining commentary which asserts: 'This is a simple memorial vid, and politics have no place here' (spelling and punctuation unchanged).[2]

Yet it is in the unregulated, irreverent, confessional nature of web-remembrance, transgressing boundaries between the formal and informal, the profane and the sacred, the public and the private, the personal and the political, which may appeal to groups who feel excluded from more traditional forms of remembrance. Who is remembered, how, why and by who is inevitably going to cause controversy and contestation – and so engagement. Arguably it should be welcomed, not silenced.

Web-remembrance has for some been a stepping stone to traditional practices of remembrance. Young people have, in recent years for example, through their Facebook sites encouraged each other to wear the traditional Remembrance Day poppy.

Notes

1 Youtube 15/9/2009 [www.youtube.com/watch?v=F1E4nsOINmQ&feature=related].
2 Youtube 19/8/2010 [www.youtube.com/watch?v=2gJnrXXumfw&feature=fvst].

The following sources were consulted in this article:

M. Aslama & M. Pantti, 'Talking Alone Reality TV, emotions and authenticity', *European Journal of Cultural Studies*, Vol. 9 No 2 (May 2006), pp. 167–84.

M. Castells, *The Rise of Network Society. The Information Age, Society and Culture Vol. 1* (Oxford: Blackwell, 1996).

RW 10-09-09, oral interview carried out in Staffordshire, 10 September 2009.

European Remembrance

WHILE the focus of this book is largely on the United Kingdom, this section explores differing approaches to remembrance that exist elsewhere in Europe. An example of the changing relationship between memory, history and remembrance is provided in relation to the Spanish Civil War; while the difficulties of coping with an uncomfortable narrative of history from the World Wars, as experienced by a defeated nation such as Germany, is also discussed. Remembrance as a culturally specific phenomenon is considered in the context of the impact of communism in the Czech Republic and pacifist memorials which commemorate the World Wars in France.

Twelve

PACIFIST WAR MEMORIALS IN WESTERN FRANCE

Dr Jane Gledhill

Those who travel widely in western France will notice that while there are English, Dutch and Belgian visitors, Germans are seen less frequently. In both the First and Second World Wars, France developed a tradition of pacifism, resistance and opposition to war. Memorials expressing these sentiments occur throughout France, but the culture of opposition to combat and of the importance of upholding peace is a tradition that is maintained in the twenty-first century in this region. In France there are forty-eight war memorials that express a pacifist viewpoint for both World Wars. In the Limousin alone there are three memorials of this kind in the villages of Gentioux, Royère-de-Vassifière and La Forêt du Temple, as well as the larger village memorial at Oradour-sur-Glane.

In the small village of Gentioux, which today has a population of 307, the war memorial stands opposite the *mairie* in the middle of the road. On the pillar fifty-eight names are inscribed, commemorating the men who lost their lives in the First World War. At the foot of the column there is a bronze statue of an orphan dressed in a school smock wearing wooden clogs. The child has a sad expression and gestures towards the names of the dead with a clenched fist. At the base of the plinth there is the inscription: *Maudite soit la Guerre*, 'Cursed be war'. The idea for a memorial of this kind was first thought about in 1922, as a result of the concern of those who fought. The initiative for the memorial was the idea of Mayor Jules Couland. He had a deep concern borne out of his experience of the war. By the end of the war his health had deteriorated because of the effects of poison gas.

Fig. 1 War memorial at
Gentioux, France.

The memorial at Gentioux never had an official inauguration. The authorities
did not recognise the pacifist character of the statement expressed through the
child's fist pointing at the names of those who had been killed. In 1922, in spite
of the refusal of the prefect to come to the inaugural ceremony, the population
of the village was united with the mayor and the Municipal Council. In an interview in a Limousin magazine in November 1971, in support of the memorial,
the then mayor said:

> Our monument to the dead never provoked discussions or arguments among
> the citizens of the commune who did not necessarily share the same political
> ideas. The cry of revolt against war simply shows the feelings of people of very
> modest conditions who were humiliated and murdered and had suffered four
> years of misery, tears and mourning.

Ten miles from Gentioux in the cemetery of Royère-de-Vassifière there is a
plaque to the memory of Félix Baudy. He was a mason who had worked on the
construction of buildings in Lyon. On 19 April 1915 he was shot at Flirey after a
unanimous refusal of his company to go over the top at the ridge of Mort-Mare.
An attack was due to take place there to destroy a trench that was still occupied
by the Germans at the centre of the front. It had been conquered a few days
earlier with a loss of 600 men. The troops for the attack had been chosen by

lot and it fell to a company that had a reputation for bravery but had already sustained heavy losses. When the signal to advance was given the troops refused to move, saying, 'It is not our turn to attack.' A few moments earlier, of the fifteen men who had just left the trench, ten had been wounded or killed in full view of their companions. General Deletoile ordered that all 250 soldiers should be court-martialled. After the intervention of the other officers, five men were chosen for a parody of a trial, two of which were chosen by lot. The other three – Antoine Morange, from Champagnac-la-riviere in Haute Vienne; Félix Baudy, from Royère-de-Vassifière; and Henri Prébost, a mason born at Saint-Martin-Chateau in the Creuse – were singled out and sentenced to death. General Joffre was aware of the decision. He was close to the battle lines at the time but refused clemency, instead demanding the greatest severity to set an example. The three men were shot on 20 April in the wood of Manonville.

Félix Baudy and his companions had their honour restored in 1934. The memorial plaque of Baudy in the cemetery of Royère-de-Vassifière, which was put in place with the support of the masons of the Creuse, has the following inscription:

Cursed be war – Cursed be its torturers
Baudy is not a coward – But a martyr

On 11 November each year those who are committed to peace come to lay a wreath on his tomb after they have gathered at the pacifist memorial at Gentioux.

In the northernmost part of the Creuse there is the small village of La Forêt du Temple which has a population of 105. Outside the *mairie* stands the war memorial. This memorial was in part paid for by Alexander Bujardet in memory of his wife Emma Marie Antonia who, as the inscription states, was 'Morte de chagrin 1917' – she 'Died of grief' after losing her three sons: Fernand (died 1915), Rene (died 1916) and Maurice (died 1915), and also her nephew Marcel (died 1915). The *mairie* accepted the donation from Alexander Bujardet and at the same time invited subscriptions from other people. Opinion from the inhabitants of the village was invited concerning the decision to have Emma Bujardet's name inscribed on the memorial. There were ninety-eight donors and only one opposed the inscription of Emma Bujardet. Alexander Bujardet was the person who took the responsibility for the oversight of the construction of the memorial. The final cost of the work was 15,500 francs. And it is clear that this was three times more than the gifts which were given by individuals. Alexander Bujardet gave the money to make up the difference.

The memorial was inaugurated on 25 May 1922, with many local officials present. However, there was some consternation expressed by the President of the Creuse Old Soldiers Association in January of the same year. He did not think that there should be a woman's name on a monument that was reserved for those men who had died for their country. He said: 'I do not think that

Fig. 2 Cars at Oradour-sur-Glane, France.

in spite of all the merit which can be attributed to the lady in question she could deserve this glorious title.' He asked if the commune could put up a simple plaque opposite the *mairie*. The mayor replied by saying that the name of Emma Bujardet figures among the four Bujardets who died for France and her inclusion in the memorial had been determined by the unanimous will of his fellow citizens. The memorial is unique in this respect in drawing attention not just to the loss of life, but to the devastating effect of those losses, and for the Bujardet family it had triggered the death also of Emma Bujardet. She too was a victim of war. The statement on the war memorial is a particular reminder of the extreme effects of grief.

The town of Oradour-sur-Glane, also in the Limousin, is a very different kind of memorial. It is not an overtly pacifist memorial but it is a powerful statement against war because of the destruction of the town and its entire population by the Germans on 10 June 1944. Originally the German command had intended that the town of Oradour-sur-Vayres should be attacked because it was thought that Helmut Kampfe, the commander of the 2nd SS Panzer Reconnaissance Battalion, was being held there.

Instead, the Germans arrived at Oradour-sur-Glane. At 2 p.m. all the inhabitants were told to go to the village green. The women and children were taken to the church and the doors were locked. The men were taken to six barns where they were machine-gunned. The bodies were covered with hay, straw and wood and set alight by the SS. The men, the dead, the dying and the wounded, were burned. One hundred and ninety men died and only five escaped. The women could hear the cries of the men but thought that they were safe. The soldiers then set fire to the church. Those who tried to escape were met with machine-gun fire and hand grenades were thrown through the windows. Only one woman survived. On that fateful afternoon 642 inhabitants were killed by the German Waffen SS Company. The village has been left as it was on that terrible day as a permanent memorial. It speaks of the tragic loss of civilian life and the horror of war. The signs in the village simply say: '*Souviens-toi*' – 'Remember'.

The Creuse is a poor area of France and traditionally there are few opportunities for employment. Men in the region trained as masons and walked to Paris or Lyon where they could be employed in construction. It was through the initiative of the Creusois masons that Félix Baudy and Henri Prébost were cleared of cowardice. Today in the church of Royère-de-Vassifière, Félix Baudy's name is on the memorial plaque, renovated in 2005. Solidarity and resistance shaped the culture of the region. It is impossible to know why the Germans razed Oradour-sur-Glane, though it was certain that Oradour-sur-Vayres was a significant centre for resistance. It was rumoured that the intention of the Germans was to terrorise the inhabitants of the region round Limoges. Today, there is a Museum of the Resistance and of the Deportation in Limoges, using pictures, archives and artefacts to keep the story of resistance alive and offer an account of the strength of opposition to war in the region.

The following sources were consulted in this article:
Gentioux: local archives in the *mairie*.
Le Monument aux morts de Gentioux [www.ldh-toulon.net].
Félix Baudy, *Maçon creusois, syndicaliste, fusillé pour l'exemple en 1915* (Publication in the Office du Tourisme).
Emma Bujardet [www.educreuse23.ac-limoges.fr].
Oradour-sur-Glane, Guide Fevrier, 1994

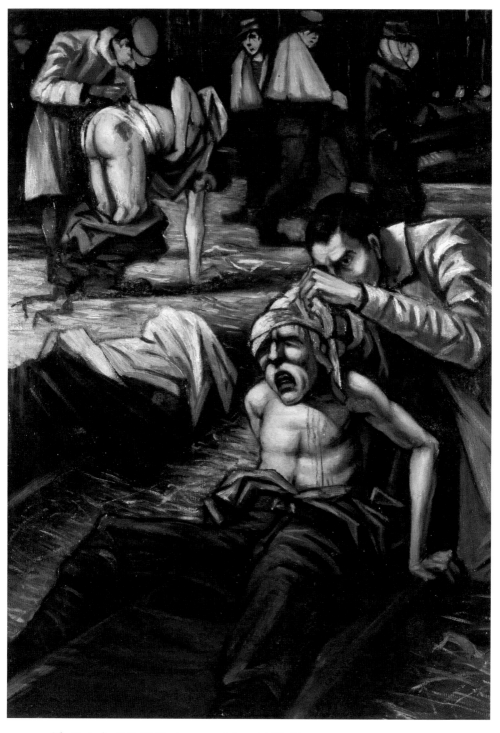

1 *The Doctor* by C.R.W. Nevinson, 1916. *Imperial War Museum*

2 *We are Making a New World* by Paul Nash, 1918. *Imperial War Museum*

3 *Toter Sappenposten (Dead sentry in the trenches)* by Otto Dix, 1924. *National Gallery of Australia, Canberra © DACS 2010*

4 *Die Mütter* (*The Mothers*) by Käthe Kollwitz, 1922–23. *Käthe Kollwitz Museum Cologne*
© *DACS 2010*

5 *Milking Practice with Artificial Udders* by Evelyn Dunbar, 1940. *Imperial War Museum*

6 *Battle of the Arakan, Men of the 7th Rajput Regiment Resting on South Hill with a Parasol Captured near the Mayu River on the Rathedaung Front* by Anthony Gross CBE RA, 1943. *Imperial War Museum*

7 Gouache from *Leben oder Theater (Life? or Theatre?)* by Charlotte Salomon, 1940–42. *Collection Jewish Historical Museum, Amsterdam* © *Charlotte Salomon Foundation*

8 *The Damned* by
Felix Nussbaum,
1943–44.
*Felix-Nussbaum-Haus
Osnabrück mit
der Sammlung der
Niedersächsischen
Sparkassenstiftung
© VG Bild-Kunst Bonn
2010*

9 *Work – sorting
out shoes,* from the
cycle *Day of a female
prisoner,* by Mieczysław
Kościelniak, 1950.
*Auschwitz-Birkenau
State Museum © The
Estate of Mieczysław
Kościelniak*

10 *In the Jungle – Guards Punishing a Prisoner, Thai-Burma Railway* by Ronald Searle, 1943. *Imperial War Museum. With kind permission of the artist and The Sayle Literary Agency*

11 *Belsen Camp: The compound for women* by Leslie Cole, 1945. *Imperial War Museum*

12 *The Boy Cornwell at the Battle of Jutland, 16 June 1916* by Frank Owen Salisbury (1874–1962).
© *Royal Naval Museum, Portsmouth, Hampshire, UK/The Bridgeman Art Library*

LIEUT GRAHAM PRICE
YPRES MARCH 9TH 1916

14 Photograph of Graham Price
from which his posthumous
portrait was painted.

15 *Their Majesties King George V and Queen Mary visiting the battle districts in France, 1917* by Frank Owen Salisbury. *Reproduced by courtesy of the Joint Grand Gresham Committee*

16 Llwydcoed Crematorium, Aberdare, Mid Glamorgan (1970), H.M.R. Burgess & Partners. *Courtesy of Professor Hilary J. Grainger*

17 Coychurch Crematorium, Bridgend, Mid Glamorgan (1970), Fry, Drew, Knight & Creamer. *Courtesy of Professor Hilary J. Grainger*

18 Durham Crematorium (1960), J.P. Chaplin. *Courtesy of Professor Hilary J. Grainger*

19 Golders Green Crematorium, London (1902–28), Ernest George & Yeates. *Courtesy of Professor Hilary J. Grainger*

20 Margam Crematorium, West Glamorgan (1969), F.G. Williamson & Associates. Distant view across Eglwys Nunydd reservoir. *Courtesy of Professor Hilary J. Grainger*

21 Oakley Wood Crematorium, Oakley Wood, Leamington Spa, Warwickshire (1971), Christopher Robinson of Sir Guy Dawber, Fox & Robinson. *Courtesy of Professor Hilary J. Grainger*

Opposite from top

22 Mortonhall Crematorium, Edinburgh (1967), Sir Basil Spence, Glover & Ferguson. *With kind permission of Mortonhall Crematorium*

23 Mountsett Crematorium, County Durham (1966), D. Kilburn of Charlton, Crowther & Partners, Leeds; view looking north towards Chopwell Woods and Hams Ferley Mill. *Courtesy of Professor Hilary J. Grainger*

And none will hear the
postman's knock
Without a quickening of
the heart.
For who can bear to feel
himself forgotten?
- W.H. Auden

Please attach your love letter to the post
box below

25   Post box, Windmill Hill, Bristol, 2009.

24   Banksy painting. Park Street, Bristol, 2009.

26 'IRAQ' street marking, St Peter's Park, Bristol, 2004.

27 'Coffin', Bristol Cenotaph, 2003.

Thirteen

RECUERDO LA GUERRA CIVIL ESPAÑA:
Turning Forgotten History into Current Memory

Dr Nigel Hunt

The Spaniards face significant problems as only now, over seventy years after it finished, have they begun to come to terms with their Civil War (1936–39). Memory plays a critical role. During and after the Franco era, people were compelled, or preferred, to forget how people in the same town or village fought on opposite sides; republicans and anarchists were terrorised for years and it is only since most participants have died that younger generations are interested in finding out more about the war. In the last few years new memorials to the victims have been erected, new museums opened, battlefields are being signposted and, after years during which British writers were seen as producing the best books about the war, the Spanish themselves are beginning to discuss the conflict.

This chapter focuses on the Battle of the Ebro, the last great battle fought by the Republican forces. The battle destroyed the army of Cataluña, leading almost directly to the defeat of the Republic a few months later. It was launched after the rebels under Franco had managed to split the Republic's territory, with Valencia, Murcia and Andalucía in the south, and Cataluña in the north still under the control of the Republic. The Spanish president, Manuel Azana, authorised the battle not because he thought the Republic would win, but to show that they could fight, and to have one last chance of getting material support from the western democracies, particularly Britain, France and the USA.

The key parts of the battle took place in a bend in the River Ebro, within which are the towns of Gandesa and Corbera. The Republicans crossed the river by night on 25 July 1938, taking key towns and villages, along with the Pandul Mountains in the south. They were stopped at Gandesa. This line moved very

Fig. 1 One of the memorials put up by the fascists, now covered in anarchist graffiti.

little for the next few months, before the rebels launched a massive offensive which forced the Republicans out of all the territory they had gained and back across the river. There were over 100,000 casualties.

Until recently there were relatively few memorials to the battle, apart from the natural memorial of Corbera del Ebro, a town totally destroyed when the rebels counter-attacked in late 1938. After the war, the people returned and, finding the town in ruins, rebuilt it lower down the hill. The ruins have since remained virtually untouched, from the roofless church to the piles of rubble that were people's houses. There are still beams jutting out into the sky, as though the destruction took place only recently. In some ways it did, as for decades the subject was not debated and the sites of battle were either built over or ignored. After the war, people spent years recovering from the destruction, and then spent many more decades ignoring the tensions and rifts within society. Franco did little to encourage remembrance and forgiveness, and it was only after his death in 1975 that people could begin to address the still-open wounds. Eventually, in 2002 COMEBE was founded to help people find missing relatives from the Battle of the Ebro (COMEBE, 2010). A Spanish law to recognise the 'individual right of each citizen to personal and family memory and its recognition' was passed in 2007. This law recognised the need to deal with issues relating to the Civil War, including helping people to find relatives buried in common graves (22296 LAW 52/2007).

The battlefield has recently seen the opening of a museum and a number of memorials have been erected, all under the title: '*Espacios de la Battalla del Ebre*' (COMEBE, 2010). Signs have been placed around the battlefield and there are tourist routes to follow to help understand the battle. The museum itself is not in a prominent position near the ruins, but hidden away at the bottom of the hill in a side street. The museum uses artefacts, descriptions and a video of people who lived in the original town during the war describing their experiences. It presents materials in a modern way, with computers showing videos and the detritus of war kept behind glass cases. Unfortunately, there is very little in English, the main language being Catalan, along with Castilian Spanish.

The original memorials at the Ebro commemorated Franco's victory rather than the people who had fought. Many of them are now defaced, often with the anarchist symbol, or by advocates of Cataluñan independence (see Fig. 1). These monuments were inaugurated in enormous ceremonies, with the victorious army dominating the public space, which helped maintain social control during the dictatorship.

The new memorials at the Ebro are dotted systematically around the battlefield. They consist of reconstructed or unreconstructed original sites of battle, such as modern metallic structures among the ruins of Corbera (see Fig. 2), reconstructed trenches (see Fig. 3), and orange signposts indicating a site of importance.

Near La Fatarella, there is a memorial to the people who fought in the battle. It is an unusual memorial, built in concrete around a trench system, where the original trenches become concrete trenches. Inside is an ossuary containing the bones of people of both sides whose remains have been found on the battlefield. Outside, there are plaques commemorating ten people who took part in the battle, from several countries, and who fought on both sides. Steps follow the trench system, emerging on top of the memorial, where there is a good view of much of the battlefield. The memorial is designed to 'transmit a feeling of understanding and reflection on death and the sacrifice of a whole generation, setting it apart from other areas meant to glorify war and its martyrs' (battallaebre.org).

Driving north through the town of La Pobla de Massaluca, heading roughly along what was the front line for most of the battle, there is much evidence of the battle: trenches and dugouts that look as though they had not been touched since the war. Beyond La Pobla de Massaluca, several kilometres along a track, there is a preserved trench and dugout system, complete with orange signs. This has recently been excavated (see Fig. 3). It was part of the Republican front-line defences during the war. There are trenches, firesteps and dugouts where soldiers lived for weeks at a time – often under fire. The Spanish landscape around here is very rocky, and often the trenches could not be dug very deep, so in order to move, a person would have to crouch down so as not to expose themselves to enemy fire. Beyond the excavated trenches one can explore trenches and deep dugouts that appear untouched since the war.

There is, unusually, a monument to the International Brigades on the battle-field. It was built in 1938, as the brigades were leaving, by British engineers and, because it is in a remote position in the mountains, it somehow escaped being destroyed by Franco's men. It was restored in 2000. It is situated in the Pandol hills above Gandesa.

Those who had fought in Franco's army might receive a pension, but the Republicans did not. For many years, thousands who had fought for the Republic were enslaved, building Franco's Spain, including the monstrosity that is Valle de los Caídos, where Franco's corpse is buried. Many areas that had fought for the Republic, such as Aragon and Andalucía, were deliberately maltreated by the new government, starved of funds, starved of food. People who were born in these areas in the years after the war still show signs of mistreatment. They are often short in stature and many have rickets and other diseases related to child-hood malnutrition.

It would not have been possible just a few years ago to even think about memorialising the Spanish Civil War in a way that represented the viewpoints of all sides, and even now there are enormous tensions. Though most partici-pants are dead, the cultural memories are still raw and unresolved; the Spanish are reticent to talk about the war. Villages and towns have divided loyalties and individuals still have resentment and anger towards those whose families were on the other side. Now, though, the Spanish are starting to look back at their war differently. The war is moving away from active memory and being turned into history. The difficulty is still that Franco was in power for so long that many

Fig. 2 This is one of a series of artworks memorialising the destruction of the village of Corbera. The ruined church is in the background and the ruins of buildings can be seen behind the artwork.

Fig. 3 These reconstructed trenches formed part of the front line for several months during the battle.

people were involved in Franco's Spain, a dictatorship that is almost universally abhorred outside Spain, but one which many people in Spain, either more or less openly, still admire and look back on with fondness.

It will be many years before Spain can look back on the Civil War without passion, though there is a clear desire to place the war in its historical context, rather than in contested memory. I have argued elsewhere that psychologically, memories of the living are transformed into history over several generations, that the children and grandchildren of participants all live with some form of 'memory' of significant events that parents and grandparents took part in. In the case of the Spanish Civil War, that transformation may take longer.

The following sources were consulted in this article:

[www.batallaebre.org/].

G. Brenan, *The Spanish Labyrinth* (Cambridge: Cambridge University Press, 1990).

N. Hunt, *Memory, War and Trauma* (Cambridge: Cambridge University Press, 2010).

P. Nora, 'Between Memory and History: Les lieux de memoire', *Representation, 26,* (1989), pp. 7–25.

G. Orwell, *Homage to Catalonia* (London: Penguin, 1938/2000).

H. Thomas, *The Spanish Civil War, 4th edn* (London: Penguin, 2003).

Fourteen

THE ROLE OF THE *VOLKSBUND DEUTSCHE KRIEGSGRÄBERFÜRSORGE* IN COMMEMORATING THE SECOND WORLD WAR

Gerd Knischewski

German memory of the Second World War is inextricably linked to the memory of National Socialism. Any commemoration is confronted with the problem of whether, and to what extent, German war memory can be separated from the memory of German expansionism, racial warfare and ultimately the genocide that came to be known as the Holocaust. As a consequence, the memory of the Second World War in general and commemoration of the dead in particular have been, and still are, far from being consensual and unifying in Germany.

This article focuses mainly on the role of the *Volksbund Deutsche Kriegsgräberfürsorge*, in short *Volksbund* or *VDK*, in official German remembrance of the dead since German unification in 1990. The name literally translates as 'The People's League for the Maintenance of War Graves'.

The *Volksbund* was founded in 1919 as a private but state-supported war graves commission, taking over the maintenance of the German war cemeteries after the German defeat in the First World War. The first central remembrance ceremony after the end of the First World War was held in 1922 in the parliamentary building in Berlin, the Reichstag. An annual national day of remembrance, *Volkstrauertag* (the people's day of mourning), was introduced in 1926.

As a result of the unconditional surrender of the German army in 1945, the trauma of total military defeat, the loss of sovereignty and a third of German territory in the east, the division of the remainder in East and West and, most of all, the moral discreditation of Germany as a result of the war atrocities and genocide, official war remembrance became a difficult matter. However, the attitudes of the Western Allies towards German war remembrance mellowed during the rapidly

Fig. 1 The central memorial of the Federal Republic of Germany to the victims of war and tyranny, inaugurated in 1993.

emerging Cold War scenario. The military administrations in the western zones, therefore, allowed the re-establishment of the *Volksbund* in the late 1940s. The Soviet occupational authorities, on the other hand, did not approve of any *VDK* activities. In 1954, the West German government re-commissioned the *Volksbund* with the task of maintaining the German war graves and cemeteries abroad.

While in the early post-war years most (West) Germans were generally reluctant to accept notions of 'collective guilt' or admit to any personal involvement in the Nazi regime and preferred to claim for themselves the status of victims, the political context changed considerably during the following decades. In the 1968 student movement, a new generation challenged the silencing of the Nazi past. The *Neue Ost-und Deutschlandpolitik*, initiated by the Social Democratic Chancellor Brandt in the 1970s, led to a climate of détente towards the East. Brandt's 1970 historic genuflection in front of the monument for the victims of the uprising in the Warsaw Ghetto was a public symbolic admission of German guilt and responsibility for the Jewish genocide in front of a world audience. The 1979 broadcast of the American TV series *Holocaust* led to countless grassroots initiatives researching local histories of oppression and resistance under the Nazis.

However, it was German Unification that had the biggest impact on the activities of the *Volksbund*. In addition to helping relatives, veterans or other interested parties in organising visits to graves, in particular on anniversary dates, it has inaugurated a large number of new war cemeteries in Central and Eastern Europe since 1990. Educational seminars and international youth camps in Germany and fifteen other countries, often held in buildings owned by the *Volksbund*, always include maintenance work on graves. Recently, the educational youth programme has been increasingly supplemented by educational services for schools, including the provision of learning materials for teachers.

Overall, the focus of war cemetery activities, and with it the financial resources involved, has shifted towards Central and Eastern Europe. After occasionally lengthy and difficult negotiations, a series of bilateral agreements were signed which allow the *Volksbund* to locate, identify and rebury German soldiers in a smaller number of new and larger cemeteries. The sheer quantity of completed work is impressive, as is its appeal to supporters. According to its website, in March 2010 the *Volksbund* had some 500,000 fee-paying members and about 1 million occasional donors. It publishes the quarterly magazine *Stimme & Weg* for its members and sponsors, as well as brochures and videos for self-promotional and educational purposes.

The *Volksbund* is the main or joint organiser of a multitude of local, regional and national annual commemorative events on *Volkstrauertag* (Remembrance Day), which was reintroduced in West Germany in 1950 under the auspices of the *Volksbund* on a Sunday in November. Since then, *Volkstrauertag* has been a national holiday with the purpose of honouring the dead of the two World Wars and, since the early 1960s, the 'victims of tyranny'.

Since Unification, and with the reinstatement of Berlin as the German capital, the central festive act has been held in Berlin, since 1999, in the Reichstag building. The live-broadcast ceremony has developed a highly ritualised pattern. The main speech is normally presented by a representative of one of the five constitutional bodies. The speeches are framed by a cultural programme, including classical music and a performance by secondary school students who recite texts such as war poems or letters from soldiers. The act concludes with the reading of the *Totenehrung* (honouring the dead). Normally, the tune '*Ich hatt' einen Kameraden*' ('I had a comrade'), which serves as the last salute to a fallen soldier, precedes the national anthem which then officially closes the ceremony.

In a country polarised by conflicting perspectives on the Second World War, the *Volksbund*'s activities have attracted criticism, mainly for its early role in shaping post-1945 West German war memory through prioritising and promoting a perspective of German victimhood. The *Volksbund* adapted to a changing remembrance culture by adjusting the motto of its work twice: 'To Our Dead' was replaced in the 1960s by 'To the Victims of War and Tyranny', and made way in the 1980s for 'Working for peace. Reconciliation over the graves'.

Since Unification of the two German states, the *Volksbund*'s activities have become much more complex; however, they still display some remarkable ambiguities. There is continuity in the way in which the Second World War is decontextualised, i.e. cut off and separated from its origin in National Socialism

Fig. 2 The memorial's centrepiece, the 'inflated' sculpture 'Mother with Dead Son' by the artist Käthe Kollwitz.

and its criminal and racist nature. Issues of responsibility and guilt, and historical explanations are largely avoided and the specific features of the Second World War are universalised, i.e. the war is seen as standing in a long line of wars before and after 1945.

Thus reconciliation (*Versöhnung*) or, more appropriately, forgiveness (*Vergebung*) becomes a principle which needs to be applied to all the fallen German soldiers, regardless of their individual behaviour. There is a strong underlying notion that all soldiers were decent young men who were forced by circumstances and hence were victims too, irrespective of the role they may have played within a murderous racial campaign. The claim that 'death has erased all differences' prevails.

Versöhnung is also attempted by a process of 'internationalisation' of the Berlin *Volkstrauertag* ceremonies, in which the *Volksbund* increasingly includes foreign guests as audience, artists or, occasionally, main speakers.

The key aim of reconciliation is attempted by the provision of facilities, activities and projects for its young members and a younger target group in general. It is in this context that the *Volksbund*'s recent slogan, 'working for peace', looks promising. The international work camps and the new *Jugendbegegnungsstätten* (young people's meeting places) are perhaps the most typical examples. Three out of the six *Jugendbegegnungsstätten* were opened after 1990. What is even more important is the fact that the work camps' syllabi and programmes often make explicit reference to the commemoration of the victims of National Socialist persecution.

As a remedy to the perceived universal evil of war, the *Volksbund* promotes a vague pacifism. One of its regular advertisements used in the past in national newspapers reads: *Mit Krieg gewinnt man keinen Frieden* ('You don't win peace through war'). However, this pacifist statement is, to some extent, undermined by the strong bonds between the *Volksbund* and the German military, the *Bundeswehr*, as a recently developing interventionist German foreign policy sees the *Bundeswehr* engaging in 'peace-enforcing' missions, most notably in Afghanistan.

The *Volksbund* faces a decline of both membership figures (owing to the ageing of its core constituency) and the public interest and involvement in *Volkstrauertag* activities, in particular local ones. However, the *Volksbund*'s role as an intermediary between official politics, army, veterans and the general public in a civil society should not be underestimated. In addition to providing legitimacy for the *Bundeswehr*, the *Volksbund* has a far-reaching socio-psychological function in disseminating socially accepted narratives, rituals, slogans and patterns of war commemoration in the wider context of coming to terms with the Nazi past. Since 1945, the *Volksbund* has quite successfully adjusted to a changing political climate without ever surrendering its focus on the suffering of Germans as victims of war.

The following sources were consulted in this article:

Volksbund Deutsche Kriegsgräberfürsorge [www.volksbund.de].

B. Niven & C. Paver (eds), *Memorialization in Germany since 1945, Section 1* (Basingstoke: Palgrave Macmillan, 2010).

Fifteen

REMEMBERING THE VICTIMS OF COMMUNISM

Kristýna Bušková

The USSR officially liberated Czechoslovakia in 1945. Following the liberation, the Czechs voted for communism in 1946 in what were to be the last democratic elections until 1990. Following the election, ideas based on Leninism and Stalinism were extended to Czechoslovakia and with it labour camps were established throughout the country for those who protested or who were viewed as threatening to the communist state. The worst times were the 1950s, when the camps became economically important. Czechoslovakia's most important export at the time was uranium, with 98,500 tons being sent to the USSR during the 1950s, mostly extracted using forced camp labour.

The people sent to camps were those accused of being involved in clandestine activities relating to the change of political regime. Of those people arrested, 262 were executed for reasons related to regime change in Pankrac prison in Prague between 1948 and the end of the 1950s – the same prison where the Nazis had beheaded 1,075 people during the Second World War. Among them was Dr Milada Horáková, a protesting democratic MP. The exact number of people imprisoned there during that period is not known.

Remembrance in relation to communism and ex-political prisoners is complex in Czech society. While Horáková is portrayed as a hero in the Czech social memory, most of the remaining ex-political prisoners are not. Instead, they are viewed as victims (compare Figs 1 & 2).

After the end of the Cold War and the fall of communism the Czechoslovak parliament passed a law rehabilitating all the people who were sentenced for political reasons during communism. It marked a breaking point from the past.

However, while it acknowledged the victims, it did not determine responsibility. Society as a whole preferred to forget communism rather than engage in remembrance and reconciliation.

After 1989 people were not initially interested in remembrance. They wanted to get on with their lives and make the best of newly presented opportunities. More recently, they have begun to commemorate and debate past events. The heroic memorial to Horáková was built and the judge who sentenced her sent to prison. Thus far (2010), this judge is the only person to have been sentenced for communist crimes.

Czech society's recognition of Horáková is in stark contrast with its lack of recognition for most ex-political prisoners. Although people agree that from 1948 onwards thousands of people worked for clandestine agencies of western states, they do not know who most of them were. Though the archives are open and there are dossiers on ex-political prisoners, it is hard to determine the accuracy of the charges. Were they really involved in clandestine activities or were they just victims of the system? We cannot be sure. The result is that society views all of them as victims. In turn, they feel unacknowledged.

Despite their official 'victim' status, Czech society is still puzzled, and old – not quite forgotten – memories from the 1950s are hitting the headlines again. Czech society feels the need to remember its traumatic past again but people are not yet properly engaging with these memories. Society is currently flooded with hundreds of stories analogously to someone who cannot control their memories of a traumatic event – and neither the participants nor society generally know how to deal with them.

Fig. 1 Memorial to Dr Milada Horáková, MP, Czech Republic.

Fig. 2 Memorial to victims of communism, Prague, Czech Republic.

Fig. 3 Key statue. *Source: www.MobilMania.cz*

In 2008 I conducted life interviews with female ex-political prisoners from the Political Prisoners Project. These interviews revealed that the moment they got into prison, political prisoners lost their status of citizens, including their right of due process of law. They described their experiences in court as a 'mockery'. Such experiences were generally incompatible with their life up to that point, as they took away its meaning. Furthermore, their existence was threatened, so to protect themselves they took a firm anti-communist stance that they never abandoned. This gave their life a new meaning: 'To be in prison gave me self-confidence. Talking politics, it convinced me that I would be against communism all my life.'[1]

In 1960, after the end of the Stalinist era, 8,708 political prisoners were released from prison under amnesty. Paradoxically, while in prison they had learned to enjoy social and intellectual support from each other, but after release they were on their own; again the meaning of life collapsed. There was no hope of getting a good job unless they agreed to co-operate with the regime, but they generally refused to accept any form of co-operation with the ruling Communist Party:

> When I returned from prison I was called by the state secret police. The police officer told me: 'You could cooperate with us. You would have all sorts of advantages.' I told him I would think about it but I was telling myself: 'You want me to cooperate with you, with such losers? You took everything away from me – health, property – and on top of that I should cooperate with you?' I did not sign anything and as a result did not get a better job.[2]

Such a stance is very different to that of a victim who is someone 'sacrificed'. Ex-political prisoners' identity became organised around their anti-communist stance and not around being a victim, independently of whether they were 'justly' in prison or were randomly selected by Communist Party officials.

Remembrance remains contested within Czech society and within the memories of the survivors. The first twenty democratic years of the Czech Republic has inevitably coincided with ex-political prisoners getting older. At this later stage of life, according to Eriksson, there is a need to achieve integrity. People want to accept events in life as inevitable and they attempt to reconcile the difficult parts. This is closely linked to the need for appropriate societal remembrance. Without this sense of integrity, older people experience despair. As part of this, social and cultural support is extremely important. Ex-political prisoners not only do not always enjoy social support, but the meaning of their lives is being directly questioned by the general public, by the culture in which they live. Their proudly presented anti-communist stance is viewed as victimhood, and as they age, they despair of achieving personal and social integrity because of this treatment, thus demonstrating the importance of sociocultural facets of remembrance.

For people in society to acknowledge the meaning of their lives they will have to reconcile with the past and accept collective responsibility for acceptance of and passivity under communism. Most people were generally loyal to the regime, though one should not forget the role of fear in the 1950s. People were overwhelmed, disorientated and many strove for mere survival, which is why this era may classify as a cultural trauma and be treated as such.

Society needs to integrate the cultural traumatic material from the communist era into a collective 'conscious' history. As Holy put it, 'in Czechoslovakia, socialism was not imposed by the bayonets of the Soviet army at the end of World War II, but grew out of the wishes of the majority of the population, to whom the justice and equality it promised seemed morally superior to the injustices and inequalities of capitalism'.

Czech society currently deals with the communist era through avoidance and labelling those who remind them of those times as victims, pushing the issue out of social awareness, and hence limiting personal growth and integrity. This, it is argued, is a cultural trauma that is equivalent to the personal response to traumatic events. As yet we understand little of what happens to a traumatised society that avoids reconciliation with its past. Can it recover? Or does society itself become a victim of its past? The ambivalence surrounding this question is expressed by a statue made entirely of keys by Jiří Černý. It is not designed as a memorial but rather a critical personal reflection of the past twenty years. The keys are those people used to rattle at demonstrations, demanding freedom. The fonts of the letters resemble fonts used in communism, and if the letter R falls off, we get the word evolution.

The statue forces us to engage in critical remembrance instead of avoidance. However, even the sculptor of this statue is over 50 years old and so it is apt to ask if the younger generation feels the need to remember. Given the increase in the number of publications on remembrance and reconciliation in the Czech Republic in the past five years, it perhaps does. Many educational activities are also undertaken, which contest the idea of remembering those who were imprisoned as victims and forgetting the communist past. Younger generations have a difficult task as they confront those – perhaps those who lived through communism – who chose to forget, and a society that has not yet recovered from the communist years.

Notes

1   Hana Truncová, ex-political prisoner.
2   Květoslava Moravečková.

The following sources were consulted in this article:

A. Applebaum, *Gulag: A History* (London: Penguin Books, 2003).

H. Ladislav, *The little Czech and the Great Czech Nation* (Cambridge: Cambridge University Press, 1996).

Art, Design & Visual Cultures of Remembrance

ART and architecture provide the usual forms of visual expression for remembrance and Christine McCauley describes the range of remembrance-inspired art that exists. This includes the intentionally striking paintings of Frank Owen Salisbury, and the simplicity of carved stones. Sometimes a counter-cultural element can exist and this is examined in the chapter on 'subvertising'. The power of art and successful architecture as a tool of remembrance can also lead to its suppression. In many crematoria, artistic form which might be considered to derive from rites of religious remembrance is frequently designed out, often leaving the buildings with a very utilitarian, if not 'soulless', feel.

Sixteen

ARTISTS OF TWENTIETH-CENTURY REMEMBRANCE

Christine McCauley

Art, informed by personal experience of war, allows the viewer to engage intimately with the human and emotional cost of conflict. Most 'official' war art reflects the values of the commissioner, whether government, military or monarch. In the past, independent responses to war, such as those produced by Goya, were rare compared with heroic scenes of battle on friezes, monuments and in paintings. Whilst political cartoonists provided an alternative to the official line, it was only in response to the First World War that a significant body of uncensored works, informed by direct experience, began to be produced and disseminated.

The First World War saw a flowering of artistic expression. The sheer scale of carnage and devastation personally involved an unprecedented number of artists, from Nevinson, Spencer and Nash on the one side, to Kollwitz, Grosz and Dix on the other. In Britain the first official war art schemes began in 1916, administered by the Foreign Office Propaganda Department. Many who became official war artists already had direct experience as soldiers or medics and had exhibited independently in shows at private galleries. C.R.W. Nevinson served with a mobile ambulance unit, producing work from 1914 onwards (see Plate 1), and Paul Nash exhibited drawings of devastated landscapes in July 1917, developed from sketches made earlier at the front (see Plate 2).

Other artists responded less immediately. It took Stanley Spencer, who spent almost four years in the Army Medical Corps and lost his brother on the Western Front, until 1923 to begin to come to terms with his wartime experiences. He said of his epic work of remembrance at the Sandham Memorial Chapel, Burghclere: 'by this means I recover my lost self.' Similarly, it took until 1923 for the German artist Otto Dix to 'somehow confront the terrible memories of the trenches' and to begin work on the fifty etchings that comprised the harrowing work, *The War* (see Plate 3).

Military service and the war's effect on civilian life led many German artists to engage in political activism and opposition. The work of George Grosz during the First World War, the 1920s and 1930s is an excoriating critique of vested interests and moral decline. Käthe Kollwitz, a political activist whose son was killed in action in 1914, articulated the impact on women, children and civilians, continuing to explore the war after 1918 when its catastrophic effect on the economy contributed to the political and social unrest that would eventually lead to the Second World War (see Plate 4).

The interwar years saw an astounding period of creative activity in Europe, principally in Germany where geographical displacement, radical politics and strong international links gave rise to movements such as *Neue Sachlichkeit* and the *Weimar Bauhaus*. Most British artists, in comparison, became inward-looking and insular as they retrenched and reacted against pre-war experimentation, many retreating into a pastoral idyll. Only in the 1930s, when émigrés from political and racial oppression in Europe began to seek refuge, did Britain once again become part of an international avant-garde.

In 1939, when the Second World War was declared, the stance of British artists was not one of protest at war's futility as it had been during the First World War, but of acceptance at its inevitability and a desire to play their part. In contrast, many German artists had their work confiscated, publicly burnt or denounced as 'degenerate' by the Nazi regime and were forced to flee to avoid persecution or internment. The British set up the War Artists' Advisory Committee (WAAC), providing employment and commissions for artists, including First World War veterans. The brief was to 'record the war at home and abroad'. Stanley Spencer was allocated shipbuilding; Eric Ravilious was assigned to the Admiralty; Anthony Gross to the War Office; and Paul Nash to the Air Ministry. The immensely varied work produced reflected the diversity of the 'WW2 experience', a global war with numerous conflict zones, types of warfare and range of military and civilian experience.

In Britain, all except two of the forty-eight women artists commissioned by the WAAC served on the Home Front. Evelyn Dunbar and Dame Laura Knight explored the effects of war on the domestic environment and women's role in the war effort. Dunbar recorded the work of women's services, including the Women's Land Army (see Plate 5). Her deadpan images transformed the domestic and everyday into surreal tableaux, whilst Knight's classic depictions and portraits of women working in manual, dangerous and previously male-dominated occupations dignifies her subjects. Policies to 'keep spirits up', and to portray women as feminine, compromised their artistic freedom but the authenticity of their day-to-day experience could not be censored and is reflected in their output.

Anthony Gross was the first official war artist to travel widely and spent much of his time with local forces on their home ground. He initially travelled to the Middle East and Syria, making studies of Arab, Indian and Syrian troops, Camel Regiments and Desert Patrols. He then accompanied the Indian army units to the Indian-Burmese border and to the front line in the Arakan and the Naga and Chin hills. There are few artistic records of the role played by soldiers from the British colonies during the Second World War, and they are largely under-represented and remembered. Gross was one of the few to record the multicultural composition of the Allied forces. He drew Gurkhas, Hakas, Pathans, Sikhs, Dogras, Chins and Naga, as well as soldiers from the Rajputana Rifles and the Lancashire Fusiliers, working on location. Rarely drawing from memory or reworking, his output was assured and perceptive (see Plate 6).

In Germany the anti-Semitic policies of the Nazi regime began to impact on the daily life of German Jews as early as 1933. Jewish artists Felix Nussbaum and Charlotte Salomon were both based in Berlin at the start of the war, but were forced to flee into hiding to avoid arrest. Their work gives us a precious insight into their lives under Nazi rule. Salomon's work, *Life? or Theatre?*, comprising nearly 800 gouache paintings with accompanying text, is autobiographical and describes her domestic life set against the backdrop of Jewish exclusion from cultural and public life (see Plate 7). Nussbaum's haunting paintings left in his Brussels studio show his mounting sense of anxiety, despair and impending doom (see Plate 8). The Gestapo discovered Salomon in Nice in 1943 and Nussbaum in Brussels in 1944. Both died in Auschwitz.

Photographs taken on liberation of the Nazi death camps in 1945 are familiar images, but there is an extensive body of work documenting conditions inside the camps dating from 1941. This was produced clandestinely under the most difficult circumstances by an astounding number of inmates; they worked on scavenged scraps of paper, hidden for fear of punishment and death. Most perished, but some who survived continued to produce work after liberation. The Polish artist Mieczysław Kościelniak was arrested in 1941 and sent to Auschwitz where he produced over 300 works. An accomplished draughtsman with an exceptional visual memory, he produced after 1945 one of the most complete, detailed and distressing visual accounts of life inside the camps in the cycle *Day of a Prisoner* (see Plate 9). Ethnic German Zoran Music was arrested in Venice in 1944 and sent to Dachau. During his year of captivity he produced nearly 100 works of the suffering, dying and dead. He survived and in 1970 began his series *We Are Not the Last*, revisiting his experiences and saying: 'If you live through that experience it becomes part of your life. And you remain forever with the corpses you left behind.'

Prisoner of war Ronald Searle recorded atrocities perpetrated on the other side of the world, after the Japanese captured Singapore in 1941. He vowed to himself: 'you are going to be an unofficial war artist and record everything that is going on.' Searle smuggled his drawings from Singapore to the camp on the

Burma/Siam Railway and ultimately to Changi Jail. He was liberated in 1945 and his book, *To the Kwai and Back*, provides a moving record of this forgotten campaign (see Plate 10). These artists' extraordinary determination to bear witness for the majority who perished constitutes an ultimate personal act of remembrance.

Those who liberated the camps included official war artists. The enormous moral and emotional dilemmas faced by artists such as Leslie Cole, one of the first to enter Belsen, took their toll later in his life. Cole unflinchingly painted the suffering and death he witnessed with great humility and humanity (see Plate 11). Earlier he had painted conditions of life under siege in Malta and later was sent to Singapore to record conditions in the Japanese POW camps.

The Holocaust personally affected artists across the Jewish Diaspora and works of 'secondary witnessing' are now being produced. Art Spiegelman, in his graphic novel *Maus*, narrates his father's struggle to survive as a Polish Jew, and contemporary artists are increasingly using the narrative medium of the graphic novel and animation to tell stories of conflict.

Traditional roles and forms of war art continue to flourish and there are still official war artists and soldier artists, some of whom record what they see through drawing and use traditional media. But the range of present-day works of remembrance is expanding and evolving. Increasingly, there are those who work conceptually, with installation, moving image and fine-art photography.

Judgements about the significance and artistic merit of works of remembrance alter over time. Work produced by artists who witnessed and recorded 'forgotten' participants or conflict zones and has emotional truth, provides an important shared experience, allowing future generations to re-evaluate, commemorate and remember.

Seventeen

FRANK O. SALISBURY 1874–1962:

A CASE STUDY IN PRACTISING REMEMBRANCE

Gill Thorn

Frank Owen Salisbury produced commemorative artwork in both World Wars: portraits, murals, stained glass and at least six First World War memorials in wood, cement, stained glass and oils. His First World War work included memorial portraits of fallen soldiers and official commissions, including *The Boy Cornwell* (see Plate 12), which commemorates an incident during the Battle of Jutland.

Wartime remembrance art is a tangible heritage, a legacy for future generations. Many of those who commissioned paintings simply wanted a lasting record of something important in the nation's or the family's history – recognisable, dignified, flattering and accurate right down to the uniform buttons. Political pragmatism dictated that while war continued, its outcome unknown, artwork should take account of the nation's morale, so there was generally little room for an artistic interpretation in an official picture. Most commissioned work has to be produced on time and in line with instructions, but war poses particular problems for the artist. Sketches may be produced on a battlefield under fire or in inclement weather; or the constraints of battle may render a general unavailable for his sitting with no time to reschedule. A memorial portrait, expected to evoke the soul of the fallen soldier, may be painted from faded photographs or even descriptions. As well as technical skill, the artist needs personal qualities of discipline, patience, perseverance, flexibility and empathy.

The son of a plumber and ironmonger, Salisbury's Methodist background and early experiences arguably contributed as much to his success as his artistic talent. Poor health meant he spent many hours contemplating life through a window, 'a constant prisoner, often looking out with longing at my brothers snowballing with their schoolmates'.[1] Methodism instilled in him the value of hard work. At 15, he was apprenticed in his older brother James' stained glass firm in St Albans. The work was tedious – grinding colours for the painters and making rough designs – but it required careful attention to detail. By 16 he was taking the place of a qualified painter and his brother sent him for formal training at Heatherley's Drawing Academy in London, where he was 'conspicuous for his zeal and ability'.[2]

His drawing master advised many years of groundwork before applying for a scholarship to the Royal Academy schools. Salisbury decided to spend his days drawing the Elgin Marbles at the British Museum and his evenings taking life classes at Heatherley's, developing organisational skills and learning to work for inspiration, rather than waiting for it. At 18 he won a British Institution award and a five-year scholarship to the Royal Academy schools. In 1901 he married Maude Greenwood. When their twin daughters were a year old, the distinguished artist and critic George Haite advised him to spend twelve months painting the twins, as it was a golden opportunity, the chance of a lifetime. While the redoubtable Maude entertained the toddlers, he devoted an hour each morning to this, learning to paint in one brief session what would formerly have taken him a week. 'Never for a moment were they still; they taught me to draw quickly, to catch a fleeting glance in a fleeting moment,' he recalled.[3] His child studies brought in commissions.

At the start of the Great War, having clocked up the 10,000 hours of practice said to make anyone stand out in their chosen field,[4] Salisbury was an established society portrait painter, operating comfortably outside narrow class boundaries and in growing demand. The war dried up this work, so he painted young combatants, some about to go into battle, others killed during battle. A painting provides a permanent reminder of the young life it honours and this poignant form of remembrance gives a special sort of comfort to an anxious or grieving family. Posthumous portraits of the fallen had to be recognisable, dignified and as flattering as public memorial art, but again, they posed particular challenges – not least that the subject could not sit for the artist; thumbnail-sized photographs or vague descriptions made it hard to capture the essence of a son or brother that the family wanted.

Lieutenant Graham Price, Salisbury's cousin, was an audacious young man who raced motorcycles at national level before the war. He became a dispatch rider in France in 1914 and finally joined the Royal Flying Corps. He received his wings in March 1916 and was killed in action six days later. There were no photographs of him in his RFC uniform as he had chosen to wait until he had his wings, so his posthumous portrait was painted using a small black and white photograph from his motorcycle racing days, the background altered to suggest an aircraft. Graham Price's sister Laura sat for the skin tones (see Plates 13 & 14).

If portraits to comfort grieving families represent private acts of remembrance, Salisbury's most commercially successful war painting, *The Boy Cornwell*, played

a significant role in national remembrance. This work commemorates an incident on HMS *Chester* during the Battle of Jutland in 1916. Jack Cornwell, a lad
of 16 from an underprivileged background, who had joined the navy without
his father's permission, remained at his post beside a gun turret awaiting orders,
though mortally wounded and with dead comrades lying around him. He was
posthumously awarded the Victoria Cross; his patriotism and dedication to duty
were to inspire the nation.

Salisbury insisted on visiting the ship to talk to witnesses of the incident, but
HMS *Chester* was always at sea, ready for action. Months after the commission a
telegram arrived summoning him to Rosyth immediately. The ship had returned
for repairs and was anchored offshore, in a howling gale. He could not set up
his easel – his canvas and palette had to be roped down – but despite the atro-
cious weather he made sketches and spoke to those who had seen the incident.
Subsequently, Jack's older brother Ernest posed in the studio as the young hero,
staunchly standing at his post.

Established artists who were unfit for active service were expected to donate
work as a demonstration of patriotism. This painting was accepted as Frank
Salisbury's 'war service'. Praised for its accuracy and technical detail, it was
widely reproduced and raised a large sum for Cornwell's Memorial Fund, which
financed cottage homes for disabled sailors.[5]

The Boy Cornwell recorded the nation's pride in its youth and conveyed subtle
messages about well-equipped ships and the courage of even the youngest
recruits. It has been criticised as a shipshape and orderly version of war, but
another event of national importance, the visit of George V and Queen Mary to
the front, was even further from reality.

This panel, commissioned for display in the Royal Exchange in 1917, is 18ft
high by 11ft wide and had to be completed in just eight weeks. The larger section depicts the king surveying the battlefields in the distance (by late 1917 artists
were banned from showing the realities of the trenches as it was considered bad
for public morale[6]). Below this, a tranquil scene shows Queen Mary visiting a
hospital, perhaps to illustrate a compassionate aspect of the battle front. The work
required a visit to the battlefields, plus sittings from all the leading figures: George
V, Queen Mary, the Prince of Wales, Earl Haig and various generals stationed at
the front. To facilitate his passage, Salisbury was given the honorary rank of colonel, with a car at his disposal and an official document authorising him to travel
anywhere – not easy in a war zone. A group of soldiers posed for sketches at the
spot where the king had stood; likenesses of the actual figures were added later
in the studio. Appointments for sittings were set up with the generals. Salisbury
was taken prisoner and escorted under armed guard to one of these; others were
curtailed as the sitter's schedule altered on the eve of a major battle.[7]

*Their Majesties King George V and Queen Mary Visiting the Battle Districts in
France, 1917* (see Plate 15) portrays an orderliness far removed from the reality of
the front, but it would be unfair to criticise Salisbury for this. Official First World

War artwork usually reflected the values of the era and the historical legacy that those who commissioned it sought to pass down. Today, democracy allows us to question elected leaders in ways that were socially impossible in 1914, when a significant proportion of the men who fought for their country were not even able to vote.

Some would argue that soldiers today are plagued with self-doubt about their role in society and that art should be about ideas rather than the end product – innovation not masterpieces. So perhaps it is surprising that some of Salisbury's meticulous work still has the power to inspire the present generation. In 2009, *The Boy Cornwell* was refurbished, re-dedicated and hung in a prominent place in St Paul's church at the training establishment HMS *Raleigh*, Plymouth. Jack's story is used to help young recruits reflect on the values of loyalty, courage and commitment; and to remind them that war is war and they will be called upon to fight.

Notes

1   F.O. Salisbury, *Sarum Chase* (London: John Murray, 1944; revised 1953).
2   B. Barber, *The Art of Frank O. Salisbury* (London, 1936).
3   Salisbury, *Sarum Chase*.
4   M. Gladwell, *Outliers: The Story of Success* (Harmondsworth: Penguin, 2008).
5   N. McMurray, *Frank O. Salisbury, Painter Laureate* (London: Authorhouse, 2003).
6   P. Gough, *A Terrible Beauty: British Artists in the First World War* (London: Sansom & Co., 2009).
7   Salisbury, *Sarum Chase*.

Eighteen

AMBIGUITY, EVASION AND REMEMBRANCE IN BRITISH CREMATORIA

Professor Hilary J. Grainger

Seven out of ten people in Britain are cremated and most people, at one time or another, attend a crematorium for a funeral service. Funerals are not only occasions to remember and honour the dead, but are also one of the ways in which we come to realise keenly the reality of our own mortality. Increasing secularisation of society has raised the profile of the crematorium to that of a highly significant public building, perhaps replacing the church as the main focus for the important function of saying farewell to loved ones. Forty years ago it was a place for cremation and a brief committal ceremony. Now the ritual, the function and the remembrance are centred increasingly on the crematorium and its gardens of remembrance – places in which many people find themselves framing their own understanding of the passage from life to death.

Britain's 260 crematoria offer an architectural form reflecting the values and social life of a modern, urban and increasingly socially and geographically mobile society,[1] yet paradoxically they remain 'invisible'. This chapter explores some of the problems faced by crematoria in providing a meaningful architecture and landscape for the mourning and remembrance of the dead.

Cremation was revived in the late nineteenth century as an alternative to burial. In Britain the movement was secular, informed by concerns over hygiene, overcrowded burial grounds and cemeteries, and supported by advances in late Victorian technology and scientific thinking. Given its long and sustained struggle against religious prejudice and conservatism, it is remarkable that cremation should have attained cultural normality, indeed ritual dominance, so rapidly by the late twentieth century. The first crematorium opened in Woking in 1889. The most recent is March Crematorium, Cambridgeshire (2010), but, significantly, two-thirds of British crematoria were built between 1950 and 1970.

Many mourners, however, find both the buildings and the process wanting. They feel 'emotionally cheated' and sometimes frustrated and uncomforted. The brevity of the service and the fact that mourners leave by a different door in order to avoid meeting the next funeral party can arguably give rise to feelings of depersonalisation, fragmentation and 'mass production'. There is also something evasive about the technology. As the coffin slides from view mourners are denied the emotional climax and finality of burial; they watch instead from a distance – passive observers rather than active participants. They are wary of what they do not see.[2] The most certain way of facing finality is to witness the cremation, which is a legal right, but very few choose to do so other than for religious reasons. In conforming to the 1902 Cremation Act, crematoria must be 200 yards from the nearest dwelling, 50 yards from any public highway and cannot be built in a consecrated part of any burial ground. Consequently, they require a disproportionately large site and are often confined to the margins of towns and cities, accessible only by car or public transport, adding further to the disjuncture in the ritual process of mourning.

Although cremation is compatible with many religious beliefs, crematoria are essentially secular buildings, often operated by local authorities serving all faiths and none, all with different but overlapping needs. At once utilitarian and symbolic, religious and secular, they are fraught with complexity. For many cremation is a religious act and so the principle determining the arrangement of a building used for a service needs to be the physical expression of a religious rite, whether this be, for example, Christian or Hindu. Ritualistic purpose must be embodied in a coherent and recognisable architectural form. For those not belonging to the dominant religious groups, their spiritual and emotional needs must also be provided for in a meaningful way. This lack of a shared and clear expectation of what is required from a crematorium has given rise to a cultural ambivalence. Unsurprisingly, architectural responses have often been ambiguous and evasive.

Two very distinct spaces are required: the functional and the symbolic, linked by a transitional space through which the coffin passes from the chapel or meeting hall to the cremator, acting both as a barrier and threshold between the 'death' and 'life' sections of the building. While the utilitarian purpose – that of burning bodies – has remained unequivocal, the search for symbolic architectural forms has proved highly problematical. Early examples were designed to look like churches, their lame Gothic style intended to offer reassurance to the sceptical and respectability to cremation through a visual connection with the Church and its tradition of burial. Thereafter, a whole variety of styles appeared. Not the least difficulty facing architects was the chimney. This did not sit happily either with Greek temples, Renaissance domes or Gothic chapels. In the majority of cases it was clear that it had been concealed within a bell tower –

a course hardly to be recommended on the grounds of truth, 'The louvres that should have emitted joyful peals often belched smoke'.[3] The majority of local authority crematoria fall, somewhat inevitably given economic restraints, into a style characterised tellingly by Alan Bennett as being 'contemporary but not eye-catchingly so; this is decorum-led architecture which does not draw attention even to its merits … This is the architecture of reluctance, the furnishings of the functionally ill at ease, décor for a place you do not want to be.'[4]

But there are crematoria that succeed in their difficult task, the challenges making them all the more remarkable. Whether by association with history, nature, landscaping or use of materials, they create a sense of 'place', a continuity and sureness in which the singular function of the crematorium is outweighed by the spiritual and symbolic resonance of the architectural language. Those that succeed in creating 'a secular version of holy ground'[5] include: Golders Green Crematorium (1902), with its simple masses derived from Lombard Romanesque; Basil Spence's quietly expressionist Mortonhall Crematorium in Edinburgh (1967), where the setting crowned by its dramatic cross invokes E.G. Asplund's Woodland Crematorium in Stockholm (1935–40); Durham Crematorium (1960), where J.P. Chaplin sought to engender a sense of history and belonging by referencing the nearby castle and cathedral in the architecture and detailing; and Coychurch, Bridgend, Glamorgan (1970), where E. Maxwell Fry reinstated the emotional value of ritual, believing that the procession of mourners through the grounds and the crematorium could itself have spiritual significance. By enriching the ceremony 'so that both it and our own lives thereby become sig-nificant',[6] Fry invoked sociologist Geoffrey Gorer, the first to suggest that those who experienced a more ritualistic form of mourning seemed able to adapt more readily to life after the funeral.

Most importantly, crematoria offered a new landscape for mourning. Cremationists were anxious to abandon the concept of the mournful, elegiac Victorian cemetery with its jostling rows of memorials, calling instead for a new setting for remembrance, a universal space of great beauty in which a balance might be struck between individual commemoration and a more collective response to the shared human experiences of loss and memory. In *God's Acre Beautiful or the Cemeteries of the Future* (1880), William Robinson argued that the alternative should take the form of a garden or natural landscape. While advocat-ing cremation on the grounds of saving space, his vision of 'garden cemeteries', in which urns would be buried, introduced a new dimension – that of the aes-thetic. At Golders Green Crematorium Robinson and architect Ernest George confined memorials to the cloisters after the manner of the Campo Santo at Pisa.

Gardens of remembrance, unique to crematoria, play a psychological, spiritual and consolatory role in shaping the human experience of mourning. The reflex-ive relationship between the living and the dead, and the interaction between a crematorium, its immediate surroundings and wider landscape, serve to create a new domain of remembrance.

During the late twentieth century many crematoria came to occupy sites of stunning beauty. Notable examples include: Haycombe, Bath (1961); Mountsett, Tyne and Wear (1966); and Oakley Wood, Mid-Warwickshire (1971). Scotland and Wales boast some of the finest locations: Clydebank (1967); The Linn, Glasgow (1962); Llydcoed, Aberdare (1970) and Margam (1969), both in Glamorgan.

Cremation raised the practical issue of the disposal of ashes, giving rise to specialised architectural features, columbaria, cloisters, colonnades and scattering lawns. Initially ashes were either buried or retained in purpose-built columbaria, but with the later popularity of scattering, columbaria were gradually replaced by walls and cloisters for plaques or memorials bearing the names of the dead. After the Second World War, other forms of memorialisation included the dedication of individual trees and shrubs. Books of remembrance were used increasingly as an alternative to *recordia* panels (wall plaques commemorating individuals), requiring halls and chapels of remembrance, often independent and placed in the grounds. The most successful crematoria are undoubtedly those that have become part of the history and culture of the communities they are intended to serve. They are linked by something much stronger than utilitarian purpose – that of offering landscapes and appropriate architectural settings ready to be invested with meaning by mourners remembering the dead.

Notes

1   For a full account of British crematoria, see H.J. Grainger, *Death Redesigned, British Crematoria: History, Architecture and Landscape* (Reading: Spire Books Ltd, 2006); P.C. Jupp, *From Dust to Ashes: Cremation and the English Way of Death* (Basingstoke: Macmillan, 2006).

2   For further discussion of problems encountered by mourners, see H.J. Grainger, 'Overcoming "An Architecture of Reluctance": British Crematoria, Past, Present and Future', in P.C. Jupp (ed.), *Death Our Future, Christian Theology and Funeral Practice* (London: Epworth, 2008), pp. 116–26.

3   J.S. Curl, *A Celebration of Death. An Introduction to some of the buildings, monuments and settings of funerary architecture in the Western European Tradition* (London: 1993), p. 310.

4   A. Bennett, *Untold Stories* (London: Faber & Faber, 2005), p. 121.

5   A. Crawford, Foreword to Grainger, *Death Redesigned, British Crematoria: History, Architecture and Landscape*, p. 12. See also D.J. Davies, 'The Scared Crematorium', *Mortality*, 1:1 (Oxford: 1996), pp. 83–94, in which he discusses the idea that for those holding religious beliefs, the crematorium and its landscape could also be 'invested with a sense of the sacred when they become closely associated with repeated memorial visits in honour of the dead'.

6   E. Maxwell Fry quoted in H.J. Grainger, '"Maxwell Fry and the Anatomy of Mourning": Coychurch Crematorium, Bridgend, Glamorgan, South Wales', in A. Maddrell & D. Sidaway (eds), *Deathscapes. Space for Death, Dying, Mourning and Remembrance* (Farnham: Ashgate, 2010), pp. 147–74; Fry, 'The Design of Crematoria', the Alfred Bossom Lecture published in the JRSA 117 (1968–69), pp. 262, 356–68; G. Gorer, *Death, Grief and Mourning in Contemporary Britain* (London: 1965).

Nineteen

'SUBVERTISING' AS A FORM OF ANTI-COMMEMORATION

Professor Paul Gough

Little is ever forgotten in Bristol. The historic enmity between the two halves of the city may be well hidden, but it is played out in the psycho-geographies of a 'federal' city. During the eighteenth century, gathered to the north around Georgian Clifton lived the high Anglican, high Tory merchant class, largely represented by the Society of the Merchant Venturers. Over centuries they became the most powerful mercantile cartel in Bristol and the region, their wealth and status partly founded on the trade in slaves and other 'goods' from the west coast of Africa. On the other side of the city were the nonconformist, Whig/Liberal industrialists of Bedminster (the separate town that eventually became south Bristol), strongly associated with dissent and the development of tobacco, sugar and chocolate industries, which were owned by nonconformist families such as the Frys and Wills – dynasties linked to the Quakers and rooted in manufacturing rather than maritime trading.

The merging of the 'Hundred of Bedminster' with the city of Bristol around 1900 brought the two ruling elites into direct competition for control of the central commemorative landscape of a new Bristol. The built environment is still bedecked with their claims to the high ground. Two edifices mark the skyline: Cabot's Tower, built in 1887, is firmly associated with the mercantile entrepreneurialism of the Italian voyager Giovanni Cabotto. A quarter of a mile away stands the 1925 Wills Memorial Building of Bristol University, which was substantially funded by the eponymous south Bristolian family and further aided by the Frys. Elsewhere in the city, other monumental forms perpetuated the adversarial frisson. In 1894 William H. Wills was returned to Parliament as MP for East Bristol, and he marked the occasion by commissioning a statue to the mid-eighteenth-century radical Whig MP for Bristol, Edmund Burke. One year later, by way of response, John Cassidy's statue of Edward Colston, paragon of the city's mercantile and Anglican values, was erected in the centre. Today, the two statues stand a hundred metres apart as a continuation of a parallel monologue in the recitation of Bristol's past. Such tensions erupt periodically but persistently. In 2006 the city held the great 'apology debate' – a mass gathering of historians, politicians and other public figures, chaired by A.C. Grayling, intending to arrive at a conclusive declaration. 'It's time the city said sorry,' proclaimed the *Bristol Evening Post*, but in the event no clear consensus emerged. On the contrary, the debate stirred up further anger and upset. Seven years earlier, with rather less fuss, Liverpool City Council had passed a formal motion unanimously acknowledging and apologising for the city's part in the slave trade.

It is not difficult to see, then, how the mnemonic landscape of Bristol offers a difficult setting for any monumental intervention. Take for example its war memorial. Given its speckled history of internecine rivalry, it will not surprise us that Bristol was the last city in Great Britain to erect its Cenotaph, a monument to the 6,000 men and women from the city who died in the Great War. Designed to unite disparate factions in one inclusive act of mourning, it was not unveiled until 1932, the delay due not to costs, design or inscription, but to its location. It stands on a traffic island on reclaimed land over the River Frome, a 'neutral' spot lodged between the mercantile north of the city and the nonconformist south – a tomb to no one on no one's land.

As major markers in the urban landscape, memorials encapsulate and perpetuate memory. The very sites and spaces they command and control are important. Rarely are they arbitrary assignations; they are 'consciously situated to connect or compete with existing nodes of collective remembering'. Containing and conveying memory, memorials exist not only as aesthetic devices but as an apparatus of social memory, as 'rhetorical topoi', civic compositions that set out our national heritage and our public responsibilities, positioned in the urban schema as the embodiment of power and memory.

However deeply submerged they may be in the collective subconscious of a city, such tensions explain why the rhetorical iconography embedded in monuments is capable of arousing such ire when they are first sited, defaced, removed or threatened with relocation. Statues, their chosen subjects and their positioning in British cities arouse passions that can seem disproportionate to the actual investment in bronze or stone. The livid protests that accompanied the erection of a statue to the RAF commander 'Bomber' Harris may seem rather extreme sixty years after the war, but that is to underestimate the role played by public artefacts in sustaining certain power bases, especially in moments of contemporary anxiety or dispute. Power, as Foucault points out, creates its own points of resistance and the power over memory and identity held by any dominant social group is rarely left unchallenged. As Morgan has argued, that which is designed to provide a locus of 'inclusion' also proclaims exclusion and can arouse disruption from a rival faction or from discontented individuals.

It is not surprising, then, that the anonymous Bristol-bred street artist Banksy chose a provocatively adversarial title for his 2009 retrospective show: 'Banksy *versus* Bristol Museum'. 'This is the first show I've ever done,' he is said to have commented, 'where taxpayers' money is being used to hang my pictures up rather than scrape them off.' Indeed, Bristol has had a 'love-hate' relationship with Banksy since he started stencilling on the city's walls in the 1990s (see Plate 24). Criticism of his state-sponsored show was anticipated, but evaporated once the queues lengthened and the acclaim spread. However, to a few discerning observers and sensitive city elders, the adversarial language rankled. It seemed to strike a jarring note in a city that had recently been short-listed for European City of Culture, where the visual arts, music, new media, film and animation had been courted, sponsored and presented as the authentic face of a city that had largely reinvented itself from an ageing port into an environmentally switched-on, culturally diverse, attractive city, hailed in 2009 as 'England's Best City to live In'. So why 'versus'? Did the phrase cause irritation because it scratched at the ill-concealed wounds in Bristol's civic memory?

Cultural historian Paul Fussell has explored these questions. He posits the confrontation between 'us' and 'them' as an example of gross dichotomising that can best be understood as 'the modern *versus* habit'. One thing is opposed to another, he argues, not in the Hegelian hope of achieving some synthesis or a negotiated peace, but with a determination that neither side should concede; that total submission of one side or the other is the only resolution.

Banksy's exhibition was clearly attuned to the historical fractures and vexatious histories of his home city. His work is aligned to, indeed perhaps derived from and nurtured by, the spirit of dissent that drives the counter-cultures of Bristol. During this same period – the tail-end of a Blair government and a Bush administration – there was increasing evidence in the city of visual dissent that drew its energy and iconography from the stencilled street art of Banksy and other street 'unknowns' (see Plate 25).

A number of these interventions took the temporary form of signs, symbols or letters painted on to road surfaces: the letter 'H' appended to the words 'BUS STOP', for example, to create the phrase 'BUSH STOP', or the outline figure of a corpse marked with the words 'IRAQ', painted on the cycle path that runs through the peace park near St Peter's church in central Bristol (see Plate 26). Other interventions appear to be more systematic. Some have a poetic air: a doomed pillar box turned into a shrine and bedecked with flowers and pleas; others are more political, many targeted at the controversial retail development Cabot Circus – a rather predictable moniker given the link between the city, commerce and capital. Guerrilla artists operating as 'subvertisers' regularly re-label and re-word billboard signs on many of their approach roads. The forms used by these interventionists are sophisticated and knowingly applied: the typography mimics the graphic conventions of corporate advertising and the wordplay links protest with politics, commerce with comedy. The same group may have been responsible in 2003 for depositing a cardboard facsimile of a child's coffin on the steps of the Bristol Cenotaph, around which were strewn bouquets of flowers, some sporting a typed label: 'For Those Who Died for Oil' (see Plate 27).

Do such gestures constitute an organised counter-culture or are they spontaneous forms of anti-corporate tagging? Are they truly contemporary manifestations of a city that is not at peace with itself or its historic past? The apology debate was inconclusive; Banksy has attained the status of canny anti-hero; Massive Attack still refuse to perform at a music venue named after Edward Colston. Should much of this surprise us? Such historical disputes mark every cityscape. In Bristol, however, they are rehearsed repeatedly in proxy through its mnemonic landscape, through the network of sculptures, statues and plinths that already litter its precincts, and more markedly by temporary and irreverent markers that shadow the official history of the city.

The following sources were consulted in this article:

M.C. Boyer, *The City of Collective Memory: Its Historical Imagery and Architectural Entertainments* (Cambridge, MA & London: MIT Press, 1996).

P. Fussell, *The Great War and Modern Memory* (Oxford: Oxford University Press, 1975).

P. Gough & S.J. Morgan, 'Manipulating the Metonymic: the politics of civic identity and the Bristol Cenotaph, 1919–1932', *Journal of Historical Geography*, No 30 (2004), pp. 665–84.

N. Johnson, 'Monuments, Geography and Nationalism', *Environment and Planning D: Society and Space*, No 13 (1995), pp. 51–65.

S.J. Morgan, 'Memory and the Merchants: Commemoration and Civic Identity', *International Journal for Heritage Studies*, Vol. 4 (2) (1998), pp. 103–13.

Regional Sites
of Remembrance

A NATIONAL desire to remember those who were killed usually develops after periods of war. Yet more local 'comradely' manifestations also develop as local communities attempt to come to terms with loss. In various United Kingdom regions, including Scotland or areas within England and Wales, remembrance activity often carries local particularities while echoing national themes and forms. However, where civil conflict has existed, such as in Northern Ireland, the forms and places of remembrance become particularly emotive and thus problematic.

Twenty

THE MAZE/LONG KESH:
Contested Heritage & Peace-Building in Northern Ireland

Dr M.K. Flynn

The former Maze Prison/Long Kesh, on the outskirts of Lisburn and 9 miles (14km) from Belfast, is one of the most controversial sites associated with 'the Troubles' (1968–98) in Northern Ireland.[1] Subsequent justifications for redevelopment as a heritage site have been hotly contested due to conflicting versions of history and identity: republican versus loyalist, nationalist versus unionist, Catholic versus Protestant. These inimical dichotomies have persisted despite the end of the Troubles and pose a question as to what and how remembering should take place. The Environment Agency's database describes historic building HB19/04/030 as a 'unique example of late 20th century emergency prison design. The Compound Prison displays the organic development of a temporary internment camp, reminiscent of WWII POW camps around the UK, into a more established structure with the concrete perimeter wall symbolising its increasingly permanent nature.' Incrementally developed during the 1970s, the prison incarcerated some 10,000 male prisoners, both republicans and loyalists,[2] before closure in 2000, although – tellingly – two of the H-blocks were temporarily left serviceable.

Despite a cross-sectarian population, including paramilitaries from all factions, the Maze/Long Kesh is associated especially with Irish republicans who took part in the 'blanket protest' (wearing only bedding after refusing to wear prison clothes), 'dirty protest' (refusing to leave cells to wash or slop out) and then the hunger strikes. This culminated in the deaths of ten republicans in 1981, notably Bobby Sands who was elected to Parliament while on strike. This seminal event, accompanied by widespread civil disturbance and intensive media coverage,

Fig. 1 Maze Prison, Long Kesh: prison watchtower.

Fig. 2 Maze Prison, Long Kesh: outside the visitors' reception.

was decisive in enhancing the political significance of the Troubles. Throughout the 1980s and 1990s, the Maze/Long Kesh remained an important presence in Northern Ireland with politics of the conflict outside the prison often intertwined with discussions and decisions undertaken within its walls, including contributions to achievement of the 1998 Good Friday/Belfast Agreement.

In 2004 ownership was transferred to the Northern Ireland Executive as one of several former security sites deemed to be publicly owned assets to be developed for the benefit of both communities and businesses. Thus the site is to undergo redevelopment to further the 'Shared Future' policy of establishing practical foundations – social, economic and political – for inter-communal trust. Indeed, the Maze/Long Kesh, 360 acres incorporating the prison and adjacent land once used for an army camp, is nearly 5 per cent of the region's publicly owned regeneration land and, as such, is the largest publicly owned regeneration site in Northern Ireland. Thus, while the politics of conflict resolution were the initial impetus for site redevelopment, resultant plans are determined by public policy emphasising provision of tangible benefits to local communities and the region. Such provision is intended not only to mitigate social inequalities and tensions, but also to counteract communal mistrust as part of fostering post-conflict relations. Hence this redevelopment involves realising a public asset as a form of peace-building for a durable post-conflict settlement.

However, the site is not just a public asset; it remains a locale of contested heritage and hence the result of redevelopment will be significant beyond material renovation alone. As the issue of historical representation stands beside that of peri-urban regeneration, the imperative is not just to renovate the site commercially, but appropriate it to redefine its meaning and use. This will mean taking into account issues related to the remembering of a violent past, with the heritage of the Maze/Long Kesh in particular standing in 'for a sense of identity and belonging for particular individuals or groups'.[3] Thus any heritage development at the site should entail consultation with a broad range of stakeholders.

But undertaking representative consultation has been problematic. Representatives from the main parties did come to a broad consensus about the site's future, as tabled in a 2006 master plan.[4] The central proposal was for simultaneous development of a multi-sport stadium, to host rugby, football and Gaelic Athletic Association matches, and an international peace and heritage centre focused around a representative sample of the prison buildings. The intention was to ensure the two projects were 'joined at the hip' so that one could not go ahead without the other.

Unfortunately, the public consultation (December 2003–February 2004) failed to provide representative input regarding site redevelopment. Not only was the consultation window open for only three months, including the winter holiday season, but results indicated that only a small number of not-for-profit stakeholder groups even took part. Of fifty-eight submissions, by far most were from individuals (59 per cent), followed by company proposals (i.e. commercial

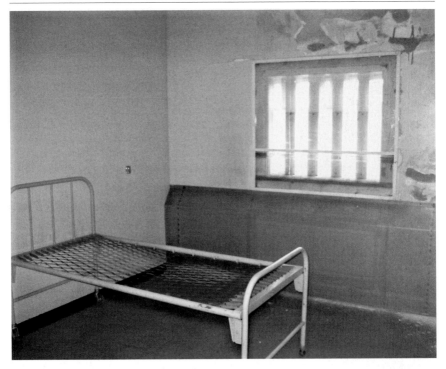

Fig. 3 Maze Prison, Long Kesh: room in a ward where hunger strikers were hospitalised.

interests) (21 per cent). Only seven (12 per cent) were from community groups, including ex-prisoners' associations. Minor input came from political parties and sports associations (4 per cent), residents' groups (2 per cent) and political parties (2 per cent).[5] A common perception was that the door for public engagement was then closed after official consultation ended in early 2004. Therefore, while the intent of consultation was to provide for stakeholder input, in practice the end of formal consultation flagged a closing to the public without establishing capacity to maintain stakeholder engagement.

Failure in inclusive practice to ground redevelopment plans on input and ongoing engagement by a range of stakeholders almost certainly destined the 2006 master plan for failure, in particular the parallel development of the multi-sport stadium and peace centre. Sometimes shrill public arguments, combined with competing parochial interests based in Lisburn and Belfast respectively, helped to defeat the stadium proposal by early 2009. This, however, still left the peace centre on the board, regardless of detractors' allegations that the result would be a republican 'shrine to terrorism'.

Strident opinions ranged from calling for a complete levelling of the site to demands for preserving much of the prison as a museum for remembrance and peace. Overseas comparisons were sometimes invoked with heritage sites and

Fig. 4 Maze Prison, Long Kesh: inside a Nissen hut used for internment.

peace centres in, for example, Argentina, the United States and South Africa. Some republicans especially pointed out the benefits of establishing a centre dedicated to reconciliation and inclusive peace education, which would have an international appeal regarding tourism, research and training, when coupled with heritage development in both a retained sample of the prison buildings and a new 'iconic' building. The project was given greater traction when the President of the European Parliament announced in November 2008 that the EU would consider helping to create the new peace centre at the Maze/Long Kesh.

In summer 2010 the Office of the First Minister and Deputy First Minister of the Northern Ireland Executive announced that it would submit 'an EU finding application for a Peace Building and Conflict Resolution Facility on the site … the centre will be a world class facility of international importance designed to strengthen our peace-building expertise and to share our experiences with others throughout the world'.[6] Thus a peace centre at the Maze/Long Kesh is slated to go forward but without its stadium counterpart. While this development will certainly be controversial for some years, past lessons regarding the divergence between the inclusive intent of the redevelopment and implementation of inclusive practice may have been learned. Unlike the past consultation exercise, efforts have been made to establish both political *and* representative stakeholder consensus before the EU application was tendered in January 2011. But if this will be enough to establish the peace centre as a permanent part of Northern Ireland's post-conflict heritage, redefining not only the use but also meaning of the Maze/Long Kesh, remains to be seen.

Notes

1   The text is drawn from a project funded by a social sciences small grant from the Nuffield Foundation (2007/08), 'Post-Conflict Settlement, Heritage and Urban Regeneration in South Africa and Northern Ireland: the Redevelopment of the Old Fort and Long Kesh/Maze Prisons'.

2   L. Purbrick, 'The Architecture of Containment', in D. Wylie, *The Maze* (London: Granta, 2004), p. 91.

3   L. Smith, *The Uses of Heritage* (Abingdon, Oxon: Routledge, 2006), p. 77.

4   Office of First Minister and Deputy First Minister (Northern Ireland), 'Maze/Long Kesh: Masterplan and Implementation Strategy (Final Report)' (May 2006) [www.ofmdfmni.gov.uk/masterplansummary.pdf], accessed 5 May 2008.

5   Annex C, Maze Consultation Panel (2005), 'Final Report: A New Future for the Maze/Long Kesh' (24 February 2005). Personal copy provided by Regeneration Division of the Office of First Minister and Deputy First Minister (Northern Ireland).

6   Office of First Minister and Deputy First Minister (Northern Ireland), 'Robinson and McGuiness announce MLK development' (29 July 2010). Personal email, 30 July 2010.

Twenty-one

REMEMBERING THE FALLEN OF THE GREAT WAR IN OPEN SPACES IN THE ENGLISH COUNTRYSIDE

Professor Keith Grieves

After the Great War some war memorial schemes commemorated the fallen on hilltops and in open spaces at sites of profound spatial relevance for nearby communities. At the summit of 'Pots and Pans' in the Pennine Hills, 259 names are inscribed on the war memorial which are arranged to face homeward in the direction of Saddleworth, Greenfield and Dobcross. An obelisk observable from almost all points of the valley stands near a druids' altar at a popular site for picnics. On Crich Hill, near Matlock, the War Memorial Tower in memory of 11,409 men of the Sherwood Foresters was unveiled on August bank holiday 1923 on a beacon site, which can be seen in Derbyshire and Nottinghamshire. In Somerset a detailed investigation of twelve hilltop sites compared the visibility of a proposed monument at each location and recommended Maesbury Castle in the Mendip Hills. However, the Shilling Fund proved disappointing and the scheme did not ensue. In each case the war memorial debates emphasised the significance of a scenic setting with a panoramic view and meaningful historical associations, which heightened the long continuities of needful sacrifice and located the memory of the fallen in beautiful countryside which was known and defended.

These civic and regimental schemes located remembrance among nature and history, to which a third dimension might be added in the form of numerous bequests of land to the nation. It is commonplace for experience of war to heighten awareness of nature. During and after the Great War, gifts of open spaces in the countryside became permanent useful war memorials to enhance life. These useful memorials have been neglected in the cultural history of commemoration and remembrance. The acquisition or provision of these amenities in the countryside on which houses would never be built became a sacred act and, like other utilitarian schemes of remembrance in towns and cities, allowed the health and happiness of future generations to inform new dignified war memorials, which were not necessarily monuments of stone. Their original purpose has sometimes been obscured by incorporation into larger schemes to preserve scenes of natural beauty in the decades which followed. The appropriateness of open spaces as war memorials was publicised in a letter to *The Times* on 7 April 1919 from representatives of the Commons and Footpath Society, Kyrle Society, Metropolitan Public Gardens Association and the National Trust. A full list of 'alternative' suggestions included woodland, meadows, recreation grounds, playing fields, common-land and footpaths.[1]

For example, in 1923 the Rev. and Mrs Somers-Cocks purchased 26 acres of Midsummer Hill in the Malvern Hills as a permanent memorial to their only son who was killed on 24 April 1918. Public access was secured and an ancient British camp on the mounded summit reminded hill-walkers of battles long ago. A refuge or 'dugout' was built on the hilltop. Permanent free access to Scafell Pike was also secured when Lord Leconfield gave the summit to the National Trust in 1919 as a memorial to the men of the Lake District who died in the war. This gift inspired the Fell and Rock Climbing Club of the Lake District to purchase twelve mountain tops for the National Trust, and to unveil a memorial, with the area depicted in bronze relief, on Great Gable in June 1924. Moorland landscapes became sites of memory and mourning as the commemoration of club members reached beyond the privileged old liberal values of property, freedom and individuality. Instead, public access to the national asset of wild mountainous terrain was secured in homage to fallen cragsmen. In the aftermath of total war, the finest views became permanent useful memorials and open spaces were rediscovered and valued because patriotism might be located in things of beauty.

These bequests and other land-purchase schemes often expressed local patriotism for the memorialisation of England's soldiers. Amid the death of landscape in theatres of war, homely scenes were remembered by soldiers. For example, Captain 'Billie' Nevill, who kicked footballs into no-man's-land on the first day of the Somme offensive to encourage his men forward, viewed the wooded heights near Amiens and imaginatively reconstructed the Surrey hills amid these foreign fields. At rest in orchards behind the front line, he also recalled peacetime visits to villages near Dorking. Remembered home landscapes were particular elements of local or private patriotisms whose pre-modern associations persisted in the Great War. In 1916 Professor William Rothenstein emphasised that everyday scenes of town and country must be seen anew: 'To see these things with the eyes of these men in the trenches is to see them more fully than ever before.'[2] This was a local world where new spiritual landmarks would connect love of beauty and useful war memorials. This 'country worth fighting for' was not a generalising 'south country' landscape beloved of recruitment propaganda, but a variegated Blighty of distinctive local scenes which was visualised from afar in the place-related memories recollected in soldiers' letters and poetry. The well-known landscapes afforded comfort and solace. They were antidotes to the nightmarish strange topographies of the Western Front, where villages vanished in an afternoon. This form of ministering romanticism was sometimes described as the propinquity of place.

In July 1919 the *Observer* strongly advocated that places of great beauty should be dedicated in memory of the fallen, and concluded that 'It is extraordinary how little of the poetry is of the war, and how much is of love for some definite part of this fair English land. Our soldier poets have turned from the desolation of war to think of the England they know.'[3] Furthermore, in the Christian tradition it is possible to view a panorama from a hilltop as God's work and contemplate life as a Psalmist might: 'I will lift up my eyes to the hills, From where is my help to come.' On 9 July 1916, Captain Adam stood on a hilltop near Etaples, joyfully amid corn and poppies, and refused to read the landscape as an infantry officer for there was no evidence of the 'military Englishman'. Instead, in the divine purpose of nature he located his life's purpose 'to teach men the beauty of the hill-sides'.[4]

By 1918 timber extraction at beauty spots for pit and trench props presumed that few large blocks of standing timber in Britain would survive the war. In contact with the Board of Trade, the National Trust sought to limit war production where the preservation of the natural and historic landscape concerned the public interest, but in 1918 the cost of war included the felling of picturesque woodland. New plantings of trees planned before the war's end evoked the call for sacrifice of men and material because they symbolised deep-rooted associations with home. The replanting of Penrith Beacon to the perpetual memory of the Cumberland lads was an example of the way that trees were perceived to mark historic epochs, and their replanting conveyed some sense of collective human and material sacrifice in the present. Consequently, land gifts often responded to preservationist fears that the speculative builder, the timber merchant and the charabanc operator would encroach on 'beauty spots' and despoil places of great natural beauty, whose vulnerability was evident in the remorseless extraction of resources on the Home Front during the Great War. It was part of the 'revaluation' of country life which occurred as social and economic certainties ebbed in rural areas in early twentieth-century Britain.[5]

The famous Surrey height of Box Hill was acquired for the National Trust in 1913 but tracts of woodland on the lower slopes were at risk from residential development at the end of the war. In 1922 an anonymous donor gave the management committee £1,000 as a 'thank offering' for the end of the war, which allowed 70 acres to be purchased. A national appeal to save Box Hill ensued, which presented the acquisition of adjacent open country as a fitting tribute to the memory of the fallen, especially for Londoners who had climbed the chalky slopes on bank holidays before the war. This appeal was successful and located within the public discourse of remembrance. Guildford Peace Day in 1919 concluded with rockets and flares sent skyward from Pewley Down, which illuminated the town. There was much public support for its acquisition as the town's war memorial to forestall building development, but the cost proved too great. However, this popular open space was purchased by Friary, Holroyd and Healy's brewery as a gift to the town in perpetuity in remembrance of the fallen. The acquisition of the Netley Park estate near Dorking by the trustees of the W.A. Robertson Bequest in 1941 was differently positioned. This private act commemorated the deaths of his two brothers in the Great War. It is one of nine gifts to the National Trust by the bequest in south-east England, all of which have a prominent commemorative stone and plaque.

There are numerous impulses in these richly textured public and private commemorative processes. Land-purchase war memorial schemes were often intensely local in design and implementation and depicted 'beauty spots' as a public asset. The schemes presumed that demobilised soldiers and their families should have democratised access to 'saved' parkland and panoramic views in 'a country worth fighting for'. This commemorative landscape was extensively depicted by Arthur Mee in his *New Domesday Book*, first published in 1936, which introduced the motorist and the rambler to the scale and diversity of memorial sites in every English county.[6] Unexpectedly, land-purchase schemes after 1918 interwove remembrance and open-air recreation in peaceful green spaces, where war experience might be more fully understood. In Armageddon's aftermath they became rather more than private haunts of ancient beauty.

Notes

1 *The Times*, 17 April 1919.
2 W. Rothenstein, *A Plea for the Wider Use of Artists and Craftsmen* (London: Constable, 1916), pp. 16–7. On 'variegated' Englishness, see D. Matless, *Landscape and Englishness* (London: Reaktion Books, 1998), pp. 17–20; R. Colls, *Identity of England* (Oxford: Oxford University Press, 2002), p. 211.
3 *Observer*, 20 July 1919.
4 L. Housman (ed.), *War Letters of Fallen Englishmen* (Philadelphia, PA: University of Pennsylvania Press, 2002), p. 21.
5 A. Howkins, *The Death of Rural England. A Social History of the Countryside Since 1900* (London: Routledge, 2003), p. 25.
6 A. Mee, *Enchanted Land. Half-a-Million Miles in the King's England* (London: Hodder & Stoughton, 1936), p. 163.

Twenty-two

NATIONAL, LOCAL AND REGIMENTAL:

COMMEMORATING SEVEN FIFE SOLDIERS WHO DIED IN IRAQ 2003–07

Dr Mark Imber

Seven young men from the county of Fife died in the Iraq War. Their names are all recorded at the Armed Forces Memorial (AFM) at Alrewas, near Lichfield. They are also entered on their regimental Roll of Honour at the Scottish National War Memorial at Edinburgh. The two other fatalities in the regiment were Barry Stephen from Scone, in neighbouring Perthshire, and Peta Tukutukuwaqa, from Fiji. The first Fife fatality recorded on the AFM is Marc Ferns. The second was Kevin McHale who died in an incident in 2004. A few entries below his name, clustered together in respect of the single incident in which they died in the deployment to Camp Dogwood in 2004, are the names of Stuart Gray, Paul Lowe and Stuart McArdle. Three years later, on a second tour of duty, the former Black Watch Regiment, by then merged as the 3rd Battalion of the Royal Regiment of Scotland, lost Jamie Kerr and Scott Kennedy in the same incident in 2007. As well as being memorialised together at the AFM and at Edinburgh, each has been accorded very different commemoration in town and parish memorials across the county. They have also been memorialised at their regimental HQ at Perth.

Names are arranged on the AFM within each service by the exact order of death. Groups of men and women who died in the same incident are therefore grouped together. The apparently random ordering of names when read by a stranger has great significance for visiting relatives, friends and ex-comrades. As occurred literally on the Western Front, so it is figuratively here; the dead 'lie' in stone amongst those with whom they died. As a UK monument, the AFM includes all Scottish fatalities. However, they are also remembered at the Scottish National War Memorial (SNWM) situated at the very summit of the Edinburgh Castle Rock and first opened in 1927. The plinth and casket containing the Roll of Honour of all the Scottish war dead of 1914–18, and all who died serving in Scottish regiments, quite literally rest on the exposed bedrock of the summit in a dedicated chapel, 'The Shrine'. The building was created from a previously existing medieval structure, its interior completely renewed as a show case of 1920s' arts and craft design. The SNWM is overwhelmingly a monument to 1914–18; when first mooted, designed and built in 1917–27 no second world war could be imagined. Just one plaque commemorates the Second World War, and the regimental Rolls of Honour, now the single Roll of the RRS, are updated to commemorate all the years from 1918 to the present. This was a conscious and deliberate decision; 'no alterations or additions were made after 1945 so that the original conception and design of the memorial should be maintained' (Official Guide, p. 3). Although a magnificent 'time-capsule' to the mass casualties and mass grief of the era, the effect is to marginalise the SNWM role as a focus of contemporary sacrifice and commemoration.

The dead of the Iraq and Afghanistan Wars have all been returned to the UK for burial. None have died unknown; none have been buried abroad. These men have, unlike those of earlier wars, been accorded both public recognition and the privacy denied to previous generations. As well as being commemorated in several public places, these men are also accorded the privacy and dignity of burial at home. Some families have combined private and public recognition of their loss, most obviously by commissioning a military style of headstone in an otherwise civilian cemetery, such as Scott Kennedy at Culross. In 2007 a new war memorial was dedicated to Marc Ferns and Stuart McArdle at Glenrothes in Fife. As a planned new town first mooted in the 1940s, Glenrothes previously had no war memorial. Two parish churches in the older villages of Markinch and Leslie had served as sites of Remembrance Day activities. Taking the form of six stone monoliths, the new memorial is located in a small open space, dissected by a footpath linking the town's pedestrian shopping mall to Church Street, the southern ring road. Six Westmorland slate monoliths recall a stone circle or ancient British henge, but divided in two halves along the central axis. Just a few metres away stands a life-size bronze statue of children at play. In addition to recording the names of the two men, a third inscription reads, 'We Honour Their Loss' and 'Let Us Not Forget'. When a town's death toll is two, it does beg the question of who the 'we' and 'us' are. Remembrance on this scale needs to be embedded firmly in local and civic culture if it is to fulfil the traditional sentiments of most 1919 memorials.

The names of Fife's other casualties of the Iraq War have been inscribed on existing war memorials in their home towns and villages across the western half of the county. Gray, at Dunfermline, has been added as one name in addition to the Second World War plaques. Kerr's name has been added to Cowdenbeath

IRAQ
Pte S. KENNEDY 28·6·2007
Pte J.W. KERR 28·6·2007
AFGHANISTAN
Cpl S.C. BINNIE 7·5·2009

BOND CL
ELLICOTT DP
McHALE KT
ROSE DM
GRAY SRT
LOWE PA
McARDLE SW
TUKUTUKUWAQA P
BROOKES SP
ANSELL MJ
NEILL DJ
CARR TA
CONNOLLY PJ

Fig. 1 Black Watch at Balhousie.

Fig. 2 Fife men at the Armed Forces Memorial at the National Memorial Arboretum.

Fig. 3 Glenrothes war memorial: 'let us not forget'.

Town Hall, McHale at Lochgelly's Main Street Kirk, and Kennedy's name is to be found at Culross. Lowe's name is carved on to the village memorial at Kelty below another single inscription, itself over fifty years old, recording the one fatality of the Korean War in 1952, which is below the massed names of over 300 from the two World Wars, marking the sacrifice of one small town. It is all the more remarkable as Kelty is a mining town, where hundreds of men would have been in reserve occupations. Newly inscribed, Lowe's name stands out from the weathered and worn inscriptions above.

A third place of memory and mourning for these men is their regimental museum, Balhousie Castle in Perth. A simple memorial to the fatalities recorded up until 2004 was erected in the grounds of the castle. It contains seven names, inscribed on the upright of a stone cross; the five Fifers are mentioned here and the names of Lance Corporal Stephen from Scone, in neighbouring Perthshire, and Peta Tukutukuwaqa from Fiji, a man recruited to the Black Watch from literally the other side of the world. The stones and inscribed rolls will endure; memorials will be passed by and sometimes read, in tandem with entirely different forms of art and engagement which also fulfil the need to remember. Gavin Burke's play *The Black Watch* may offer the soldiers immortality in the Scottish school curriculum, whilst a brief account of the circumstances of these fatalities, and of every death of the UK military in Iraq, can be found in Nicol's account of the Iraq War published in 2008.

Fig. 4 Lowe at Kelty.

Tracing the memorials for the seven soldiers from Fife thus serves to empha-sise that the casualties of war are members of national, local and regimental communities and there is consequently a need for their deaths to receive public recognition within each of these different cultures of remembrance.

The following sources were consulted in this article:

G. Burke, *The Black Watch* (London: Faber & Faber, 2007).

M. Nicol, *Iraq: A Tribute to Britain's Fallen Heroes* (Edinburgh & London: Mainstream Publishing, 2008).

O. Oliver, *Not Forgotten* (London: Hodder & Stoughton, 2005).

The Scottish National War Memorial, Official Guide (Edinburgh: SNWM & Jarrold Publishing, 2004).

Twenty-three

FATES, DATES AND AGES:

An Investigation of the Language of War Memorials in Three Regions of Britain

Colin Walker

There is no doubting the physical presence of many war memorials. Walter suggests that in suburban London, with the absence of a 'natural focus like a village green or old parish church … the memorial to those who died in the First World War became a focal point'.[1] The language displayed on war memorial inscriptions also has the potential to create an impact upon onlookers. This chapter draws upon discourse analysis, which explores 'how … written language is used in social contexts',[2] to discuss the emergence of a language of remembrance after the First World War, inscribed on war memorials in three regions of the United Kingdom – the north of England, mid-Wales and central Scotland.

In the first of these regions an especially revealing inscription is found within St Andrew's churchyard, South Otterington, North Yorkshire, which categorises those touched by memorials with the words: 'To the living – gratitude. For the dead – remembrance. For posterity – imitation.' Not surprisingly, virtually all of the inscriptions discovered in the three regions studied refer to remembrance of the dead. A slight variation of a very popular inscription, and one immortalised by Rudyard Kipling, can be found at Purston, West Yorkshire, reading 'Their Names Liveth For Evermore'. In Llwyngwril, Gwynedd, a typical Welsh inscription records '*Yn anghof ni chânt fod*', or 'They will not be forgotten', whilst the more common version of the first inscription, simply, 'Their name liveth for evermore', can be found at Forth, South Lanarkshire.

Many inscriptions refer specifically to men, such as in 'honoured memory of the men connected with the village' at Midgeley, West Yorkshire. Nevertheless, a recognition of the contribution made by women can also be found, such as

Fig. 1 South Otterington, North Yorkshire: the agenda is set.

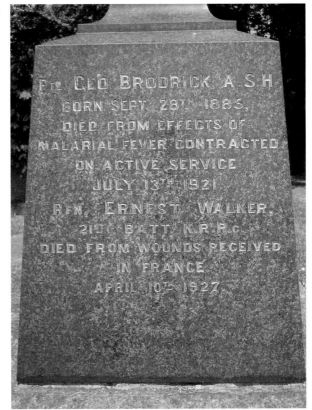

Fig. 2 Amcotts, Lincolnshire: remembrance of the fate of the dead.

ERECTED
BY THE PEOPLE
OF CRAWFORDJOHN PARISH
IN MEMORY OF THE MEN
WHO FELL IN THE
GREAT WAR.

PTᵉ HUGH DILLON A.&S.H.,
ACCIDENTALLY KILLED IN FRANCE
30ᵗʰ SEPT 1939.

FORGET WE NEVER OUR HEROES AND MARTYRS

Fig. 3 Crawfordjohn, South Lanarkshire: gratitude from the living.

on the park inscription in Greater Manchester, which reads 'In Remembrance of the men and women of Dukinfield', and at Llanwddyn, Powys, which details the 'men and one nurse from this parish [who] also served in H.M. forces'. In Carmichael, South Lanarkshire, reference is made on the Roll of Honour to one nurse in the Malayan Auxiliary Services. More noticeably, regional differences emerge in the use of 'terms of endearment' on inscriptions. So, reference is made in Lincolnshire to the 'fifteen Wadingham Lads who fell', whereas at Coedpoeth, Wrexham, credit is paid to 'the gallant boys of the parish of Bersham'. Meanwhile, two inscriptions at Lesmahagow Cemetery, South Lanarkshire, recognise 'Servants of God, well done'.

References to the parish feature consistently on inscriptions in all three regions, whether it be 'to the heroic men from the parish of Allerton Bywater' in West Yorkshire, or 'in grateful memory of those from this parish' at Llanddwywe church, Gwynedd. In South Lanarkshire there is recognition of the 'ever loving memory of the men of the Parish of Culter'.

The declaration of values such as sacrifice features within many inscriptions, albeit allowing for subtle differences in the emphasis placed upon language employed across the regions. So, at Thurstonland, West Yorkshire, the inscription reads: 'Their Sacrifice shall Live for Ever.' On the Roll of Honour inside St Mary's church, Llanfair Caereinion, Powys, a more personal tribute is given in the form of the words 'paid the supreme sacrifice', which are entered in red alongside the names of men who served in the First World War. At Elsrickle, South Lanarkshire, warm acknowledgement is made of 'Two gallant heroes who sacrificed their lives'.

Many inscriptions reveal details which may be characterised as 'Fates, dates and ages'. So, for example, in Amcotts, Lincolnshire, specific reference is made to a soldier who 'died from the effects of malarial fever contracted on active service', whilst at Llanllwchaiarn, Powys, there is an accurate record of the fate of another soldier 'who fell at Ypres 24th October 1914'. It is quite common to also acknowledge those who served and returned, and not just the fallen. So, a typical Welsh Roll of Honour is to be found in Llanerfyl, Powys, headed '*Rhestr or rhai fun gwasanaethu*', or 'Served and returned'. Meanwhile, in Douglas cemetery, South Lanarkshire, a single grave adjacent to the main war memorial has registered the details of a private who died from his war wounds on 16 January 1920, aged 42, but whose name is not recorded on the main Roll of Honour.

Again, and not surprisingly, many of the inscriptions discovered in the three regions studied refer to gratitude on the part of the living. A minor alteration is

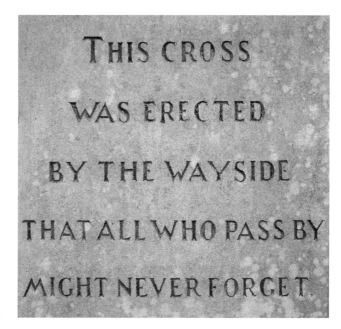

Fig. 4 Eastoft, Lincolnshire: a message for posterity.

made to the most common English example of inscription to be found within this category at Gringley-on-the-Hill cemetery, Nottinghamshire, in the form of 'Lest We Forget'. Meanwhile, a somewhat warmer tone is set through, for example, the inscription at The Royal British Legion Club in Llay, Wrexham, which reads 'Forever in your debt'. By way of further contrast, a highly positive tone is set through the use of the words on the inscription 'Forget we never our heroes and martyrs' at Crawfordjohn, South Lanarkshire. Such sentiments are reinforced in all three regions by more specific reference to memory. So, for instance, at Middleton in Teesdale, County Durham, an inscription simply records: 'Erected in grateful memory of the fallen.' In Wrexham, the statement offers heartfelt thanks and is more localised by way of the words: 'Erected in grateful memory of the men of Pentre and district.' As is the case in South Lanarkshire, where acknowledgement is made through the words: 'Erected to the memory of the men of Forth and district.'

Across all three regions, inscriptions record that sense of commitment to commemoration by way of local communities declaring their funding sources. So, although in Kirton in Lindsey, Lincolnshire, the inscription declares that 'This monument was erected by public subscription, Sept. 26th 1920', at Middletown, Powys, the simpler message 'erected by public subscription' can be found. Likewise, in South Lanarkshire an inscription merely records: 'Erected by the public of Pettinain.' Nevertheless, it is not just accreditation of the general public which appears on inscriptions throughout the three regions in question; parishioners also make strong claims. Allerton Bywater, West Yorkshire, acknowledges their role simply with the inscription 'Erected by parishioners 1920', whereas in Chirk, Wrexham, a more personalised accreditation comes by the use of the words: 'This monument was established by their fellows of the Parish.' At Elsrickle, South Lanarkshire, an even more intimate sense of parishioner recognition is encapsulated in the inscription 'Erected by members of Ellsridgehill U.F Church, in memory of these who fell'.

Although least numerous, it is those inscriptions making reference to the desire for imitation by posterity which arguably prove to be the most revealing in all three regions studied. Recent plaques recording restoration work carried out are quite common and display the extent of local pride involved in the very maintenance of those village war memorials concerned. So, for instance, in Lincolnshire one such plaque informs visitors that a war memorial has been 'Maintained in gratitude and remembrance by Crowle & Ealand Regeneration Group'. Direct references to passers-by can also prove to be interesting and informative, such as the one inscribed on a war memorial plaque at Eastoft, Lincolnshire, which reminds them that 'This cross was erected by the wayside that all who pass by might never forget'. By contrast, at Maentwrog, Gwynedd, the entry gate to the war memorial site is simply inscribed 'Sedd gyhoeddus', or 'Public seat', representing a clear invitation to passers-by to spend a little time in order to reflect. An even more direct invitation to do just that can be found in Crawford, South

Lanarkshire, on a war memorial inscription informing passers-by 'Here are six names to remember'.

Thus, studying village war memorial inscriptions makes it possible to recognise the phenomenon whereby, in the wake of the First World War, a 'language of remembrance emerged that enshrined the experience of the war'.[3] This language is exemplified by the Roll of Honour inside Christ Church, Appleton-le-Moors, North Yorkshire, which reads: 'Courage to resist. Patience to endure. Constancy to persevere.'

Notes

1   T. Walter, 'War Memorials', in S. Mumm (ed.), *Religion Today: A Reader* (Milton Keynes: The Open University, 2002), pp. 116–7.

2   D.E. Gray, *Doing Research in the Real World* (London: Sage, 2nd edn, 2009), p. 576.

3   G. Parsons, *Religion Today: Tradition, Modernity and Change Perspectives on Civil Religion* (Milton Keynes: The Open University, 2002), p. 43.

National Remembrance Events & Places

T HIS section explores the establishment of a national culture of remembrance in the United Kingdom after the First World War – including the Cenotaph, the poppy and the two minutes' silence. It also examines some recent changes to national commemoration, including the effects of the creation of the Armed Forces Memorial at the National Memorial Arboretum in 2007. The need to promote a broad understanding of the importance of remembrance in a largely 'demilitarised' age as being taken forward through the educational work of The Royal British Legion and other charities, including The Holocaust Centre, is also discussed.

Twenty-four

THE CENOTAPH AND THE SPIRIT OF REMEMBRANCE

Philip Wilson

Monuments, memorials and graves provide a tangible link with the past and create a place of pilgrimage, an environment for remembrance. However, the spirit of remembrance is all around us in cities, towns, villages, rural communities and in the many battlefields across the world; and many of the rituals and artefacts associated with remembrance in this country grew organically, and almost accidentally, in the aftermath of the First World War. Remembrance is thus not restricted to local war memorials and inscriptions, but has many other facets, and it has helped to shape communities in the United Kingdom over many years. Remembrance is also personal; it takes many shapes and forms, and memories can be stirred when least expected.

In Britain the act of wearing a red poppy, the two minutes' silence to remember the dead, ceremonies and parades at the Cenotaph in Whitehall and The Royal British Legion Festival of Remembrance at the Albert Hall have contributed to a shared culture of grief on Remembrance Day. The ceremonies that take place on 11 November, and the nearest Sunday to it, were initially conceived to mark the anniversary of the end of the First World War, the first truly mechanised and mediated war. War by its very nature is cruel and the Great War touched diverse and divergent societies in many different ways. Each combatant nation suffered grievous losses. With very few exceptions, the dead were buried where they fell on the Western Front, or in faraway places like Gallipoli, Salonika, Mesopotamia, Palestine, Italy, Africa and Russia, to name but a few.

In October 1914 Fabian Ware and Dr Stewart, a Red Cross medical assessor, visited Bethune Cemetery. On seeing a number of British graves with their plain

Fig. 1 The Cenotaph prior to it being unveiled by King George V. *Imperial War Museum*

wooden crosses, Stewart suggested that although they were adequately marked, there seemed to be no evidence they had been recorded or registered and so the task commenced. Whilst every effort was made to give proper burial to those who were killed in action, with graves being marked by either a wooden cross or a frail memorial, these were often obliterated by successive bombardments. By early 1915 it was recognised that the practice of burying British soldiers in local civil cemeteries in France could not continue and so land was purchased for military cemeteries. The horticultural work commenced in 1916 with the help and advice of the Royal Botanical Gardens at Kew. Plants and seeds from Kew were sent to France through funds supplied by the Red Cross. Nurseries were set up and some of these, including many cemeteries, were overrun and destroyed as the war raged. Throughout the conflict and turmoil of the Great War the spirit of remembrance was kindled by the significant losses experienced.

Edmund Blunden in *The Immortal Heritage*, written in 1937, recalls that in 1917:

the idea that these battlefields would themselves ever become pasturelands with grounds and lakes and garden walls would have appeared sheer fantasy. Those who experienced the horror of the trenches on the Western Front lived from day to day and those who stopped to reflect often felt that their death would be nothing short of a complete and final disappearance. Little wonder that many men succumbed to shell shock, serious injuries, including blindness from gas attacks.

Those who sought solace in writing poetry or letters home added yet another dimension to the war; their published diaries and poems often reveal the futility of war and total destruction experienced by those who took part.

Following the Armistice on 11 November 1918 the key rituals and practices of remembrance which are familiar in contemporary society were quickly developed. At a national and a personal level, those who had survived tried to manage the multiple narratives of the destruction and carnage of the First World War. Immediately after the First World War ended, work commenced on the permanent cemeteries and within a few years these beautiful gardens of rest appeared. By 1920 pilgrimages, individual and collective, had also commenced and the then Imperial War Graves Commission began its long association with the newly formed British Legion in 1921 and the travel agents Thomas Cook.

As the first anniversary of the Armistice drew near, the Cabinet received a request on 4 November 1919 that the Armistice be commemorated by a silence, along the lines of the three-minute silence observed at noon each day in Cape Town during the Great War. The Cabinet agreed and King George V issued a personal request that at the eleventh hour of the eleventh day of the eleventh month there may be a brief space of two minutes, a complete suspension of all our normal activities. The shared silence came to operate as a junction between private memories and public rituals in the years after.

The origins of the present Cenotaph in Whitehall lie in a temporary structure made of wood and plaster and designed by Sir Edward Lutyens, at the request of the then Prime Minister David Lloyd George, for the Peace Procession in London on 19 July 1919. At a historical juncture where unemployment and labour unrest were growing, the government regarded the attitudes of both serving and demobilised members of the armed forces with some anxiety. The Peace Procession, the temporary Cenotaph and a celebration of the successful end to the war were intended to encourage national solidarity. The word Cenotaph means an empty tomb in Greek and was intended to symbolise and remember the fallen; it captured the public imagination as repatriation of the dead had not been allowed. Bereaved widows and families spontaneously heaped flowers at its base after the procession had passed; it symbolically stood in for the graves of their relatives. Little wonder there was a public demand for a permanent stone structure.

The present Cenotaph in Whitehall is an exact replica of the temporary structure, undecorated save for a laurel wreath and the inscription at each end, 'The Glorious Dead', chosen by Rudyard Kipling. It is flanked on each side by various flags which Lutyens had wanted to carve in stone. Constructed from Portland stone by Holland, Hannen and Cubitts, its sides are not parallel, but if extended would meet at a point some 300m (980ft) above the ground. Similarly, the 'horizontal' surfaces are in fact sections of a sphere whose centre would be 270m (900ft) below ground. It was unveiled in its permanent form by King George V at exactly 11 a.m. on 11 November 1920, two years after the First World War ended. For over nine decades it has acted as the focal point for national, official remembrance services in which political dignitaries participate on the Sunday nearest to 11 November.

A further acknowledgement of the difficulties faced by those whose relatives' bodies had never been identified was the burial of the Unknown Warrior which followed the unveiling of the Cenotaph. A gun carriage containing the coffin of the Unknown Warrior – chosen from four unknown servicemen killed early in the war in Aisne, the Somme, Arras and Ypres – made its way to Westminster Abbey, followed by the king, Field Marshal Haig, General French, Admiral Beatty, the king's ministers and a vast throng. The main body of the Abbey was largely given over to war widows. Following a brief service, the Unknown Warrior was lowered into his grave near the Great West Door. In a day filled with symbolism, the grave was refilled with earth brought from the battlefields. Over 40,000 members of the public filed past the tomb before the doors of the Abbey closed that night.

The appropriation of the poppy as a symbol of remembrance the following year was prompted by Madame Anne Guerin, who encouraged the newly formed British Legion to use it to raise benevolent funds through the annual Poppy Appeal. John McCrae's poem 'In Flanders Fields', written during the Second Battle of Ypres in 1915, had drawn attention to the poppies which grew amongst the debris of battlefields. In 1917 the Somme battlefield was apparently a blaze of scarlet with patches of yellow charlock and white chamomile. The poem had had a profound impact upon a young American, Miss Mona Michael, who bought twenty-five artificial poppies to be worn in memory of the fallen at a YMCA Conference in 1918 and went on to launch a campaign to make the poppy the symbol of remembrance. It was first adopted by the American Legion in 1920 and Britain in 1921. The poppy quickly became the very essence of the spirit of remembrance, worn by all at the Cenotaph. The Royal British Legion's charitable work, which poppy sales continue to fund, has endured for ninety years and will continue for many years to come.

The British Legion's first Festival of Remembrance was held in a packed Albert Hall on the evening of 11 November 1927, with 10,000 be-medalled veterans each wearing a Flanders poppy, their faces hardly visible through the haze of tobacco smoke. The Band of the Grenadier Guards played old wartime songs and the veterans sang themselves hoarse by the time the final tune, *Tipperary*, had been reached. The proceedings concluded with the Prince of Wales making a short speech. Led by the prince, the whole audience then left the Albert Hall, to march to the Cenotaph in a torch-lit procession, the immense column being joined at Knightsbridge by veterans who had listened to the proceedings in Hyde Park.

The national significance of each of these rituals and ceremonies rested not merely on the activities in London. Throughout the 1920s, all across the UK war memorials were unveiled in villages, town centres and cities commemorating the names of the fallen. On Remembrance Day, as the sounds of the eleven chimes in Whitehall faded away and the assembled crowd observed the two minutes' silence, simultaneously crowds were gathered at local war memorials across the land. Furthermore, in the 1920s and 1930s the wireless broadcast the remembrance service, live from the Cenotaph on Armistice Day, enabled the ceremony and the two minutes' silence to become a truly national event. Individuals within their homes shared this public event, able to feel a sense of identification with those at the Cenotaph. Many others in the following weeks watched recordings of Remembrance Day ceremonies in cinemas where the ceremony at the Cenotaph, the Festival of Remembrance and the national sharing of two minutes' silence would take up a whole newsreel.

In the twenty-first century, over ninety years after the end of the First World War with but two surviving British veterans of that conflict, the poppy, the Cenotaph, the two minutes' silence and the British Legion's Festival of Remembrance remain part of the annual tapestry of remembrance in November each year. They are accompanied by a plethora of other acts of remembrance at national, local and personal levels shared by television, the press and the internet. Their meanings and significance are multiple, shifting and contested at both a national and personal level; the public desire for these rituals of remembrance expressed in the 1920s seems unabated.

Twenty-five

MEETING A NEED?

What Evidence Base Supports the Significant Growth in Popularity of the National Memorial Arboretum?

Charles Bagot Jewitt

With a mission to be the UK's year-round centre for remembrance – a spiritually uplifting place which honours the fallen, recognises service and sacrifice and fosters pride in the country[1] – the National Memorial Arboretum has within ten years established itself as the most significant centre for remembrance in the United Kingdom, outside of London. This is complementary to the Cenotaph which remains the national focus for national remembrance ceremonies in November each year.

Centrally located in the Midlands, with over 7 million people within a one-hour drive, the Arboretum was founded by David Childs,[2] a retired naval commander, who was concerned that the debt owed to his parents' generation was insufficiently commemorated nationally. He was inspired by the Arlington National Cemetery and the National Arboretum of the United States, near Washington DC. The original objective was to commemorate those who had lost their lives in the wars of the twentieth century, together with a strap-line of 'Remember the Future' to encourage future generations not to repeat the mistakes of the past. The wish was to commemorate and to move on from the twentieth century – probably the bloodiest period in the history of mankind.

With the dedication, in the presence of Her Majesty the Queen, of the Armed Forces Memorial in 2007, a significant national memorial to those who have died in military service in the country since the Second World War, visitor numbers at the Arboretum quickly rose from 60,000 to approximately 300,000 per annum and have remained around this level for the last three years. This caused the Arboretum to revise its objectives to include those serving in current

Fig. 1 The stretcher bearers. The Armed Forces Memorial at the National Memorial Arboretum, Staffordshire.

Fig. 2 Visitors at the National Memorial Arboretum.

Fig. 3 The 'Ride to the Wall' event at the National Memorial Arboretum.

conflicts. The Arboretum has also embraced organisations with a national need for remembrance beyond the military, including civil services and charities such as the Royal National Lifeboat Institution. The current strap-line, 'where our nation remembers', reflects the site's increasing national importance and a sense of place.

Visitor figures and comments collated from visitors would seem to indicate that the Arboretum is meeting a need, but further questions may be asked about 'what need or needs?' and 'will these trends and needs continue into the future?' The use to which the Arboretum is put is instructive in this regard. It is more than a 'visitor attraction', attracting large numbers by car, bus and coach for a day out. It is also a focal point for remembrance services and reunions for over 200 organisations that represent themselves through memorials or plant-ings on the 150-acre site. Some of these are big events: the Korean veterans muster over 3,000 people, and a motorbike rally known as 'Ride to the Wall' attracts around 10,000. Additionally, educational, spiritual and other social activities, such as those delivered through the Arboretum's Friends organisa-tion, draw many to the site.

In late 2008 the Arboretum carried out primary research through an internet survey. The information gathered was used to underpin a projection of future visitor numbers by tourism consultants who sought to ascertain the likely size and characteristics of the population of potential future visitors. The survey was not based on those who had visited but on a statistically robust population who responded to a description of the Arboretum and subsequent questions which

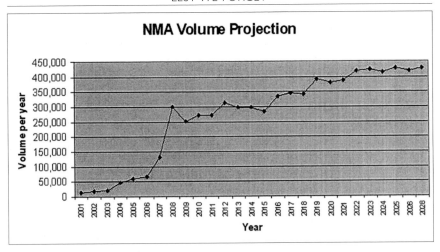

investigated a propensity to visit. This was to provide a sound underpinning for the forecast of visitor growth to 415,000 per annum by 2023 shown above.

Unsurprisingly, the survey revealed that people with a 'military' connection, which was interpreted very broadly to include the civil services (police, fire, ambulance), were far more likely to visit than those without. Also, this population was heavily skewed towards older people. Half of the under-35s could think of no one in their family of any generation associated with the services. Generational distance from someone who had served was measured and the conclusion drawn that the likelihood of visiting fell away according to generational distance, likelihood to visit being strongest in the current generation and weakening one and two generations removed, reflecting Britain's progressive demilitarisation.

On the face of it, therefore, the Arboretum could expect a gradual reduction in visitor interest over the coming decades. However, the research went on to indicate that other elements of the National Memorial Arboretum's visitor proposition could be used to engage with visitors going forward, potentially enabling the interest of future generations to be sustained.

While the research placed the Arboretum as a fairly typical 'military' site, ranking it ninth on a list of fourteen well-known visitor attractions, just behind the Imperial War Museum, Duxford, it also revealed that the appeal of nature-based sites was significantly higher than military ones. This presents the Arboretum's management with both an opportunity in broadening the appeal of the Arboretum as a world-class landscape, such as Kew Gardens, Stowe or Stourhead, but also a challenge in not alienating the core military-associated customer base.

Attitudinally, although younger people were more 'fun' focused, 46 per cent of respondents agreed that 'it is important to remember people and events in the past', and 40 per cent agreed that 'our country is shaped by ordinary men and women as well as famous people'. These assertions, and a statement that 45 per cent say they are likely to visit a place if it is 'free to get in' (which is true of the

National Memorial Arboretum), provide an indication that there are potentially many who would be interested in visiting if the context of the Arboretum is presented more broadly than purely as a memorial site.

So what are the limitations of this research? Firstly, coming so soon after the dedication of the Armed Forces Memorial, the research probably did not reflect the growing importance of the Arboretum as the national focus for contemporary (as opposed to World War) remembrance activity – evidenced by the 2010 dedication of names ceremony on the Armed Forces Memorial, which gained widespread live media coverage, or the dedication of the Basra Memorial Wall in March 2010, which was attended by all the political party leaders. Daily conversations reveal that the site has undoubtedly gained enormous emotional importance among people bereaved as a result of service, many of whom make numerous visits and feel an attachment to the place far stronger than would be felt with less unique visitor attractions. This may explain why a high percentage of repeat visitors, approaching half the overall number, is revealed in the Arboretum's own visitor surveys.

The design of the Armed Forces Memorial has also become widely appreciated nationally; perhaps unusually for a modern piece of architecture, it has attracted no controversy and is clearly becoming iconic to many. The number of organisations wishing to gain recognition by placing a memorial at the National Memorial Arboretum site, some forty-four on the current list, also provide testament to a growing appeal among the various 'tribes' of the nation that the different memorials and plantings on the site represent. Indeed, recent additions such as the Polish memorial are significant sculptural works in their own right and add to the momentum for further visits to view the latest developments. So how has the National Memorial Arboretum reacted to this primary research? The Arboretum's response has been in three main areas.

In terms of the current visitors' needs, the Arboretum has already extended its existing facilities to cope with additional numbers and there are plans for further extensions to help ensure its future commercial and financial viability as a largely self-supporting entity while maintaining free entry. Moreover, the research has assisted the Arboretum, and its parent charity, The Royal British Legion, towards an understanding of the importance of engaging contemporary society and in presenting the concept of remembrance to visitors and to future generations through the Arboretum site. A Remembrance Learning Centre, including state-of-the-art visitor 'interpretation' and learning facilities, is currently in design and has been subject to a further feasibility study.[3] The centre would provide a prime environment for The Royal British Legion to deliver much of its learning programme, which is closely linked to the citizenship syllabus in schools; and the study concluded that 'a site of this stature needs and demands first class interpretation and there is a danger of not providing good interpretation on the site'.

The enduring and popular appeal of world-class landscape attractions which the research highlighted has led to the creation of a renewed Landscape Master

Plan for the site, and a focus on developing the landscape experience in the context of other landscape grand designs. Many memorial sites across the world are set in magnificent surroundings: Arlington in the USA; the Australian National War Memorial in Canberra; Verdun and many Commonwealth war grave cemeteries in France and Belgium. Such sites have significant appeal, aesthetically as much as for the memorials they contain, and this appeal is both international and enduring through periods of relative peace. The National Memorial Arboretum needs to see itself and develop in this context to achieve its recently stated vision of being a 'world-renowned Centre for Remembrance'.[4]

Finally, the generational issues highlighted by the research have assisted the Arboretum and The Royal British Legion in considering the wider issues of remembrance and the need to keep the concept fresh and contemporary through changing generations. A world where widespread interest in family antecedents is evidenced in the popular television programme *Who Do You Think You Are?*, and in which deaths of servicemen are announced through the Facebook social-networking site, would be scarcely imaginable a decade ago. It is vital that the Arboretum continues to promote research and understanding into remembrance – a concept probably as old as mankind but which changes its form decade by decade, culture by culture – to keep relevant to current and future generations. This volume, as an output of the recent series of remembrance seminars at the Arboretum, represents a significant start to the process.

Notes

1   NMA Business Plan, April 2010.
2   D. Childs, *Growing Remembrance, The Story of the National Memorial Arboretum* (Barnsley: Pen & Sword, 2008).
3   The BDRC survey was based on a sample size of 1,000 adults aged 16 or over who lived within a two-hour drive of the Arboretum postcode (DE13 7AR). The respondents were recruited through Aurora Market Research's online panel. Half the respondents were within a one-hour drive time radius and half within two hours. The survey was divided into four life stages: pre-family (adult under 45 years without children in the household); family (adult with children in household); working grey (adult over 44 years without children and in work); and retired (self-defined, without children in the household). Each sub-segment was selected to be representative of the UK population by age and gender. October 2008 [www.bdrc-continental.com].
4   Britton McGrath Associates [www.brittonmcgrath.co.uk].

Twenty-six

THE FUTURE OF REMEMBRANCE IS OUR YOUNG PEOPLE

Paula Kitching

The media frequently assert that young people know little about history and therefore pay scant attention to the sacrifices of those who served in the major conflicts of the twentieth century. Some believe that schools deliberately drop aspects of remembrance from the national curriculum for fear of offending specific groups. The experiences of the learning team for The Royal British Legion (TRBL) do not, however, support these assertions. This article explores the positive experiences of TRBL's learning team among young people and how young people can engage enthusiastically with national remembrance events.

When TRBL was formed in 1921 it took on two mandates: welfare for veterans and their families, and remembrance. Prior to the First World War the concept of a period of annual national remembrance, such as we have today, did not exist. The unprecedented scale of that conflict meant that many in the population had lost family or friends, and most people had known someone who had served or participated. As Wilson recounts in Chapter 24, a popular demand for a collective day to remember developed – originally on 11 November, the date of the signing of the Armistice, and later on Remembrance Sunday. Once TRBL adopted the poppy as its symbol of remembrance, one day and one symbol became the standard practice.

Ninety years later, the UK is no longer a country shaken by mass warfare. Although military operations have continued to the present day, no conflict since the Second World War has significantly impacted on civilian lives. Throughout this period, the population has expanded and diversified and the welfare work of TRBL has continued in support of servicemen and women who serve and have served. However, for some the act of remembrance has become remote and attached to a previous generation. Media reporting of the recent conflicts in Iraq and Afghanistan has reminded people of the reality of war, but the contested politics surrounding these conflicts can leave people, and perhaps especially young people, confused about what remembrance is for and what its associations are.

Describing itself as the nation's de facto custodian of remembrance, TRBL takes every opportunity to raise the awareness and to promote reflection upon the significant sacrifice the country's armed forces make, both in past and present conflicts. Over the past ten years this has included finding new ways of engaging young people. The object is not to target young people for Poppy Appeal fundraising, but to connect their lives with remembrance and to encourage their active participation. The approach embodies a central message of TRBL: that it is not war and conflict that is remembered, but the people whose lives are affected by war and conflict. Through this approach, TRBL would like all young people to have the opportunity to learn about its charitable work, the significance of the poppy and to participate in an act of remembrance.

Over a decade ago, TRBL successfully campaigned to have remembrance placed on the national curriculum. In the years that followed it has developed a large outreach programme based on a suite of print and digital materials and resources for both schools and informal educators. TRBL's target has been not just youth organisations that might already be sympathetic to the remembrance message, such as cadets or scout groups, but young people right across Britain. Each year the resources are updated, incorporating factual material that supports the national curriculum. Lesson ideas and case studies of real people encourage students to investigate the lives of those affected by conflict and war, and to engage in local research, using databases, exploring archives and researching war memorials. A range of information is provided to teach them the effect that conflict has on servicemen and women and civilian populations. Sources include film and personal testimony, maps, pictures, poetry and documents.

Workshops and conferences are also held for young people to explore remembrance from multiple perspectives. Opportunities are provided to allow students to examine their own attitudes to remembrance and to discuss topics such as 'how we remember', 'who is remembered' and 'what is reconciliation?' Young people are introduced to the distinction between personal forms of remembrance, such as learning about a family member or taking a moment to reflect on one person, alongside collective forms of commemoration, such as attending a remembrance service or simply wearing a poppy in early November. Activities are designed to suit different age groups and abilities and to promote not only knowledge, but creative responses that reflect a real understanding of the topic. In this regard, younger children often like to draw existing memorials or to design their own; older groups may be stimulated by the harrowing poetic imagery of Wilfred Owen or Isaac Rosenberg to write their own poetry.

Fig. 1 School children and veterans at the Dunkirk commemoration, 2010.

Fig. 2 Student at a Second World War Commonwealth War Graves Commission (CWGC) cemetery in France.

Fig. 3 School children laying a wreath at a remembrance event in France for the Dunkirk commemorations, 2010.

Poppy Travel, TRBL's travel arm, has also developed tours for young people led by specially trained staff. These tours not only enable young people to visit memorial sites but also to participate in their own acts of remembrance where they lead and lay a wreath. Significant memorial sites are visited across the UK and Europe, from trenches to cemeteries, and in recent years this has included the National Memorial Arboretum, which includes education as part of its mission and where TRBL is currently extending its learning programme. Enabling young people to have input on remembrance events can inspire and provide them with the confidence and desire to repeat their involvement.

TRBL's learning materials and websites also address such issues as the roles of women in conflict, from the Home Front to their mobilisation in military operations, enabling young people to appreciate how conflict can affect everyone in society. Young people are almost invariably interested to learn about ethnic, religious and national diversity within the UK armed forces, which has been a feature of the British military over many decades. The challenges and experiences of Walter Tull, a black soldier recruited into the British army during the First World War, are featured in the 2010 TRBL learning pack. The discovery on a Poppy Travel trip to Ypres of a Muslim name next to a Hindu name on the Menin Gate caused one British Muslim teenager from London to admit that his attitude changed from 'what has this got to do with me' to 'how can I find out more?' And to ask 'can we say a Muslim prayer at the cemetery?'

An effective method of engaging young people can be to ask them to select a name when visiting a memorial or cemetery and ask them to be 'responsible for remembering' that name. Giving remembrance such a personal context, especially if backed up by research on the individual or the knowledge about the conflict in which the person fell, allows the two minutes' silence to take on a much deeper meaning for young people who have not personally known family or friends affected by war. The laying of a wreath to that person can be even more powerful. If, say, grandparents have fought in conflicts, then the effect can be inspirational, and feedback to TRBL indicates that otherwise underperforming children can connect to their grandparents' generation through the study of memorials, and be stimulated to encourage their parents to take them on visits to memorial sites and to lead assemblies in order to pass on where they have been and what their connections are.

Whenever possible young people are introduced to veterans, as cross-generational dialogue can enhance the leaning experience, often for both groups! In

Fig. 4 British school boy in a CWGC cemetery on the Western Front as part of a school tour.

this context veterans may be from the Second World War and in their eighties or in their twenties and newly returned from Afghanistan. The exchange of experience, the understanding of the grim reality of warfare and the conversation engendered is almost invariably more engaging than the history of a particular conflict. For young people, the veterans are the physical embodiment of some of those things they have learned. For the veterans, an element of reassurance exists that their experiences are of interest to others and will be remembered beyond their own families. TRBL has also introduced the concept of asking school children to write to veterans' families and injured service personnel; in some instances this has had a significant impact on the development of understanding between the two groups.

So TRBL's aim is to promote widespread understanding of remembrance among young people and to ensure their active inclusion in commemoration. The more that young people are invited to take part or, even better, to help organise a remembrance event, then the more likely it is that remembrance will assume greater meaning for each individual. Through remembrance study can become a considered response to the tragedy of human conflict; and although the format and formality of remembrance ceremonies will change with each generation, the national tradition started in 1919 will, assisted through education and learning, remain alive and pertinent for many years to come.

Twenty-seven

'THE JOURNEY': A UNIQUE APPROACH TO HOLOCAUST EDUCATION

Karen Van Coevorden

The 'H' word, Holocaust, is one that is often avoided in primary schools for fear of causing distress or alarm. Yet, is this really a valid excuse for dismissing this period of history from the curriculum? Or is it possible to teach about the systematic murder of 6 million Jews in a sensitive and age-appropriate manner? Opened in September 2008, 'The Journey' is the UK's first primary school exhibition dedicated to teaching about the Holocaust. Created by Dr Stephen Smith, founder of The Holocaust Centre, 'The Journey' uses survivor testimony, film, photographs and artefacts to tell the journeys of Jewish children who lived through the Holocaust and survived or who escaped from Nazi Germany before the war began. In this chapter, I will outline the pedagogical approach adopted in 'The Journey', discussing in detail the methods we use to engage and enthuse students in an exploration of this difficult area of history. I will explain how the Holocaust can be taught from a young age by providing examples of age-appropriate activities which are both challenging and meaningful.

'The Journey' tells the story of Leo Stein, a fictional Jewish boy whose narrative is based on the experiences of a number of survivors living in the UK. By focusing on one character, a child the same age as the Year 6 students that visit the exhibition, this is a reminder that the Holocaust affected individual people and lives; large statistics are often difficult to comprehend. The initial film introduces Leo to the students: he lives with his family and has a happy home life but recently things have started to change. Adolf Hitler is now the leader of Germany and he is making life difficult for the Jews. Leo's story unfolds through his diary and a series of rooms showing home, school, street, shop, hiding, carriage and refuge.

Fig. 1 The first room in 'The Journey' exhibition: a typical 1930s German-Jewish home.

Fig. 2 The street in 'The Journey' depicts the damage caused during the November 1938 pogrom.

Clockwise from above

Fig. 3 Each artefact in 'The Journey' tells a story. The block of gold concealed inside this brush helped secure Simon's safety while in hiding.

Fig. 4 2 December 1938: Leo, the main character in 'The Journey', embarks on his journey to England.

Fig. 5 A montage of images found in 'The Journey'.

As the students enter the first room, a family dining room, they are transported back in time to the 1930s. In this space, a hands-on experience is encouraged and the students are allowed to touch and play with the objects. There is something for everyone and this approach engages all learners, visual, auditory and kinaesthetic. It's Friday evening and the table is set for a Shabbat meal – you can even smell the chicken soup that Leo's mother has prepared! While some students reach for the challah and candles, others choose to play with the cars and dolls in the toy box, try on the fur stole or read Leo's diary. The home depicts everyday life and this is further reflected in the short films describing survivors' memories: Dorothy recalls birthday parties, while John talks about his dog, a black chow. This inclusion of special celebrations and pets, often key aspects in any child's life, are an important reminder that the survivors too came from loving families and had happy childhoods. A focus on Jewish life in Europe before the war is vital when delivering Holocaust education as it helps students to understand Jewish people in the context of life and community rather than solely as victims.

School occupies the majority of any child's day, so the classroom should be a familiar environment, but Leo's treatment by his teacher is not typical. In his diary, he recalls: 'The teacher told everyone that I was Jewish … She pointed to my nose, my ears, my hair and my chin. Everyone thought it was very funny and laughed – but it wasn't very funny for me.' Several students may have experienced bullying and be reminded of this after hearing Leo's words, but obviously we encourage visitors to reflect on how the teacher's actions are different from what we would expect.

The November 1938 pogrom, Kristallnacht, is depicted through a series of vandalised shops in a street. In an attempt to understand the reason for this attack on the Jewish people, the students listen to Leo's diary, but the bigger questions still remain about why ordinary people and especially the firemen did nothing to help. While the terms 'bystander' and 'perpetrator' are not specifically referred to, it is important that even at this young age the students are aware that people had choices about their behaviour. Discussion in this space centres around 'who' is responsible and a clear distinction is made between 'Nazis' and 'Germans'; while many of the Nazis were Germans, not all Germans embraced Hitler's regime. Correct use of specific terminology is encouraged as this avoids stereotyping (against the Germans, in this instance) and ensures historical accuracy. A bench in the street indicates *NUR FÜR ARIER* (only for Aryans), a reference to one of the many anti-Jewish measures that were enforced on the Jewish people before 1938. While discrimination of this kind is difficult to comprehend, an effective way for today's students to begin to understand these restrictions is by reflecting on how the Jewish people might have felt when they were forbidden to sit on park benches or banned from the cinema. Learning always has a greater impact when the concepts are tangible and students are able to place the experiences within their own realm of understanding.

After the November pogrom street scene, the final rooms of 'The Journey' are connected with the choices made by Leo's family, who eventually decide to send him to England on a *Kindertransport* (children's transport). Around 10,000 children arrived in the UK as part of this scheme; many were never to see their families again. Leo's journey ends in safety, but not all children were so lucky. While 'The Journey' does not aim to shock or traumatise, there is a need to present an accurate portrayal of history and this therefore must include mention of the other journeys that were made at a much later date, many to ghettos and concentration camps. December 1938 may mark the end of Leo's journey but for other Jewish children, theirs had not even begun. With the outbreak of war, as new countries came under Nazi rule, the lives of many more thousands of Jewish children were in danger. Short films in the carriage reflect some of these experiences. Steven, a survivor from Amsterdam, recalls travelling to a ghetto in Czechoslovakia:

> We embarked upon a journey which was about 39 hours, which I shall never forget. No food, no water, no sleep, and this terrible stench of sweat, human sweat 'cause it was September '44, of vomit, faeces (that's poo), urine (pee), all mixed in together, and it was almost as if the oxygen was being starved out of the air, you could hardly breathe … And we'd arrived in Theresienstadt, Terezin.

Regardless of age, it is inappropriate to expect students to imagine or understand what this journey was like. While role-play activities should be avoided, the murder of 1.5 million Jewish children cannot be ignored. Gas chambers do not need to be spoken of or graphic images shown; we do not need to focus on the method of murder but should spend time learning about the individuals who died for no other reason than being Jewish. In 'The Journey', where we are working with younger students, we do not want them to leave feeling traumatised by the experience; the final room encourages a detailed study of the personal objects that our survivor speakers have donated or loaned, enabling the students to add further meaning to what they have learned.

Student reactions to 'The Journey' are often reflective and thoughtful. Many speak of contemporary issues such as bullying and racism, and although we aim to teach about the Holocaust itself, it is interesting and noteworthy that students personally draw out these issues. A visit to 'The Journey' ends with a survivor giving their testimony. Personal testimonies are a powerful way of enabling students to relate the Holocaust to the lives of an individual; the ability to engage and ask questions of the survivor allows them to seek further insight into their life. Knowing that they have had a personal encounter with an eyewitness of the Holocaust can be a life-changing experience and students are often empowered to effect change in their life: 'I found the survivor's story one of the most powerful ones I've ever heard and I will try my hardest to try and stop anything like that happening again in the future' (Elizabeth, age 10).

Although the Holocaust did not happen long ago, to the young students that visit 'The Journey' this period is often viewed as ancient history. So why is it still important to teach about these horrors? What relevance does it have for young people today? The answer is simple: we continue to educate about the Holocaust because it is an unprecedented event; it is the first time in history that a nation systematically planned to murder an entire group of people on a global scale. For this reason alone, even younger students should be taught something about how and why this event occurred. It is important to mention that the perpetrators were not monsters or psychopaths, but ordinary people, like you and I. These people did not act alone; murder on such a large scale was only made possible by the collaboration of neighbours and friends of Jewish people. The Holocaust therefore challenges our views of human behaviour and perhaps also makes us reflect on ourselves so we feel confident and empowered in our learning to play our part in ensuring such atrocities are not repeated again.

The Holocaust did not begin with mass murder. It began with a deep-rooted history of anti-Jewish feeling; anti-Semitism still exists today, as does persecution towards many minority groups that are perceived to be 'the other' or 'different'. While the main aim of 'The Journey' is to teach about the Holocaust, students often leave the centre challenged to consider how the consequences of their own actions impact on the lives of others in their schools and local communities today.

By the end of 'The Journey', it is hoped that the students will have gained a deeper understanding of the historical events of the Holocaust and the personal experiences of Jewish children during that period. For the majority of students, the most memorable part of their visit is meeting the survivor; having listened to their testimony, the students become part of the legacy and have a duty to share what they have learned with future generations. This challenging task is a responsibility for us all.

Women & Remembrance

WOMEN have tended to be marginalised from traditional memorialisation and military-focused acts of remembrance, but there is a long tradition of remembrance activity in women's culture. This activity may be politically motivated, as in relation to the death of the suffragette Emily Wilding Davison, or in women's writing during the First World War. The struggle for recognition of the female contribution and sacrifice in wartime is exemplified in the chapter on widows' pensions and in the recently constructed memorial commemorating the role of women in the Second World War, erected in London, the design of which has been contested. Remembrance is now perhaps more inclusive, partly because of the changing role of women in the armed forces.

Twenty-eight

WOMEN'S WRITING AND THE FIRST WORLD WAR

Dr Jane Gledhill

Women's response to the First World War was multifaceted and contradictory. Women gave out white feathers to men who had not enlisted at Christmas 1914; at the same time many women tried to get their sons out of the army, and other women agitated to prevent conscription. On 27 April 1915, at the Women's International Conference at The Hague, it was agreed that delegates from the Congress should go to 'belligerent and neutral governments and the president of the United States' to demand peace. At the end of the war, 16 million had been killed. Women responded to the First World War with a rich mix of both unpublished and published writing, many examples of which can be found in the Imperial War Museum's extensive archive of letters, diaries and memoirs. These writings, together with published poetry, novels and autobiographies, provide a woman's voice in First World War remembrance.

A number of the letters home from women near the front played down the effect of war; for example, Dorothy Higgins wrote: 'I don't think you have to be so melancholy about the Verdun attack: the huns are losing men in thousands and gaining very little for it.'[1] She went on to say that she would be taking leave: 'I shall prune all the roses and spend your birthday with you which shall be ripping.' At the time she was working in a hospital in Rouen dealing with horrific injuries, but there is no mention of suffering in her letters. In London the writers who were later seen as shaping modernism – Hilda Doolittle, Virginia Woolf, T.S. Eliot and D.H. Lawrence – determined that although they were not at the front, they should continue to write with the same dedication as if they were part of the war effort. This was described by T.S. Eliot as 'a continual self-sacrifice, a continual extinction of personality'. In any reading of Hilda Doolittle's poetry, the stark imagery reveals that death was just below the surface, as her poem 'Loss' demonstrates:

> One of us, pierced in the flank,
> Dragged himself across the marsh,
> he tore at bay-roots
> Lost hold on the crumbling bank.[2]

In *Mrs Dalloway* Virginia Woolf traces the impact of Septimus Warren Smith's shell shock through to the end of the novel and his eventual suicide.[3] Her treatment of death and loss in *To the Lighthouse* is contained in a middle section of the book entitled 'Time Passes', which is a reflection on the death of Mrs Ramsay and also describes the death of her son. This is put in square brackets to emphasise the loss: [a shell exploded; twenty or thirty men were blown up in France, among them Andrew Ramsay, whose death, mercifully, was instantaneous.][4]

Vera Brittain, who wrote *Testament of Youth*, left Oxford after one year and became a VAD in the summer of 1915. During the war her fiancé, Roland Leighton, two other friends, Geoffrey Thurlow and Victor Richardson, and her brother, Edward Brittain, were killed. Her book begins by describing the summer of 1914 when she went to the speech day at Uppingham. She records the headmaster's statement: 'If a man cannot be useful to his country he is better dead.'[5] It has often been remarked that these words reinforced the urgency of enlistment encapsulated in the phrase '*dulce et decorum est pro patria mori*'. When Vera Brittain wrote *Testament of Youth* in 1933, she remembered the Uppingham speech day as a 'perfect Summer Idyll' and wrote: 'The lovely legacy of a vanished world. It is etched with minute precision on the tablets of my memory.' The process of remembering had been a way of confronting the unimaginable loss inflicted by the war, and understanding how it had shaped twentieth- and twenty-first-century culture. When Vera Brittain died her will stated that her ashes should be scattered on her brother's grave in the Italian village on the Asiago Plateau. She reflected that 'for 50 years much of my heart has been in that Italian village cemetery'. The loss of her fiancé made her ask a particular question in her poem 'The Superfluous Woman':

> And far away,
> Behind the row of crosses, shadows black
> Stretch out long arms before the smouldering sun
> *But who will give me my children?*[6]

For women after the war who lived with grief and loneliness, remembrance became an important way of ensuring that the loss had not been in vain. Three diaries written by Irene Rathbone, which formed the basis of her semi-autobiographical novel, *We that were Young* (1932), provide further examples of this and are kept in the Imperial War Museum. She reflected on the war:

> The dawn came slowly, the great blackness of night split into greyish clouds which in their turn became fiery red till the whole sky was ablaze with crimson – threatening, terrible [after the night's events]. I remember staring out with a little shudder, sheer terror gripped me for a few moments – war, war. What might it not mean – this was the blood of gay, splendid youth drenching the sky to that dreadful colour.

Towards the end of her diary she wrote:

> I think I have now put down everything that is of importance, or that I want to remember in the days when the War burst upon us so swiftly, that there was no time to think of reasons before it had caught us all in its cruel grip to be crushed and moulded by pain into very different people from what we were in those careless far-away days which we call 'before the war'.[7]

A different kind of remembrance was expressed in Rebecca West's novel, *The Return of the Soldier* (1918), which deals with the effects of shell shock and loss of memory. Forgetting, for many, became a way of remembering. *The Return of the Soldier* described how the war punctured the structures of British society. Baldry Court was a house full of 'brittle and beautiful things', and there Kitty, Chris Baldry's wife, and the narrator, Jenny (Kitty's sister), waited for Chris to return. Their serene environment was set in beautiful English countryside: 'miles of emerald pasture-land lying wet and brilliant under a westward line of sleek hills blue with distance and distant woods.' It is Jenny who holds the image of Chris close to her and imagines how it must be for him in action:

> By night I saw Chris running across the brown rottenness of No Man's Land, starting back here because he trod on a hand, not even looking there because of the awfulness of an unburied head, and not till my dream was packed full of horror did I see him pitch forward on his knees as he reached safety – if it was that.

Jenny's love for Chris is more palpable than Kitty's. She lives out his pain as a soldier in the night hours. However, the reality of Chris' experience broke into Jenny and Kitty's life through Margaret Grey, who brought news that Chris was suffering from shell shock and had lost his memory: "'He isn't well! He isn't well!'" she said pleadingly. "'He's lost his memory, and thinks – thinks he still knows me.'"[8]

His memory had blanked out the past fifteen years and he remembered only that he had loved Margaret first of all. The central irony of the novel is that Margaret, with her cheap stays, 'deplorable umbrella' and 'unpardonable raincoat', should cut through social convention and reach beyond the cool formalities of the upper middle classes to Chris' heart. Jenny, Kitty and Frank, the cousin, an Anglican chaplain at the front, stand on the edge of Chris' life. It is Margaret who penetrates the centre: 'The whole truth about us lies in our material seeming. He sighs a deep sigh of delight and puts his hand out to the ball where Margaret shines.' Jenny can see that his cure rested with Margaret; while her spell endured they could not send him back to the hell of war: 'This wonderful kind woman held his body as safely as she held his soul.' Margaret enabled healing for Chris through reminders of his past and of his young son who died. He returns to the house cured, and 'Every inch a soldier'.

Research, appraisal and publishing work written by women about the First World War continue and more recent anthologies of poetry, for example *The Penguin Book of First World War Poetry*, include poems by a number of women. For many people – especially children studying English literature in schools – poetry provides a significant introduction to contemporary cultures of remembrance. In this collection, women's work complements and offers commentary on the poems written by men. Sir Henry Newbolt's celebrated poem 'The War Films', which opens with the line 'O living pictures of the dead', comes after Teresa Hooley's poem 'A War Film', where she describes watching a film of the Mons retreat and then returning to bathe her little son:

How could he know
    The sudden terror that assaulted me? …
    The body I had borne
    Nine months beneath my heart,
A part of me …
If, someday,
It should be taken away
To War. Tortured. Torn
Slain.
Rotting in No Man's land, out in the rain –
My little son …
Yet all those men had mothers, every one.[9]

Notes

1 Imperial War Museum Archives.
2 H. Doolittle, *Collected Poems* (Manchester: Carcanet, 1984).
3 V. Woolf, *Mrs Dalloway* (London: Granada, 1983).
4 V. Woolf, *To the Lighthouse* (London: Penguin, 1964).
5 V. Brittain, *Testament of Youth* (London: Fontana, 1970).
6 G. Walter, *The Penguin Book of First World War Poetry* (London: Penguin, 2006).
7 I. Rathbone, *We that were Young* (London: Chatto & Windus, 1932).
8 R. West, *The Return of the Soldier* (London: Virago, 1980).
9 G. Walter (ed.), *The Penguin Book of First World War Poetry* (London: Penguin, 2006).

Twenty-nine

SUFFRAGE, SPECTACLE AND THE FUNERAL OF EMILY WILDING DAVISON

Dr Maggie Andrews

On 14 June 1913 a funeral procession, three-quarters of a mile long, preceded a memorial service at St George's church, Bloomsbury, for Emily Wilding Davison – the suffragette campaigner who had died as a result of injuries gained when she ran on to the track of the Epsom Derby in front of the king's horse. Her fellow suffragettes in the Women's Social and Political Union (WSPU), who were consummate publicists, reportedly marshalled 6,000 women to accompany the coffin, followed by: an empty carriage for the rearrested Mrs Pankhurst and one with Davison's mother and Davison's 'intimate companion'; brass bands; members of the clergy; and banners pronouncing 'Fight On and God will Give Us Victory'. The spectacle of public mourning – which has been likened to a 'mobster's farewell'[1] – produced a range of images which adorned the pages of the world press and were viewed in perpetuity: on newsreel in cinemas and now via YouTube, arguably creating the blueprint for political funerals in the mass media age.

The practice of turning a funeral into a spectacle was by no means new, and has been utilised for celebrity military leaders such as Nelson and Churchill. Wellington, whose defeat of Napoleon at the Battle of Waterloo (1815) evoked hero worship, despite an unsuccessful period as prime minister, justified a massive funeral procession: a four-and-a-half-hour journey across London for the hearse and a plethora of poetry including Tennyson's ode on the 'Death of the Duke of Wellington' (1852). This may be seen as 'a yearning to render into public spectacle the unseen', defiled, indefinable and tabooed object of the corpse,[2] but the scale of Victorian and Edwardian funerals – Queen Victoria's utilised more troops than took part in the first expeditionary force to the Western Front in 1914 – was also an assertion of the deceased's power, significance, wealth and, in the determination to avoid a pauper's grave, respectability.

Funerals, like other acts of remembrance, assert a sense of community and belonging, to family, region and class, to the nation and empire in the funerals of Wellington and Queen Victoria, and to the suffragette cause in the funeral of Emily Wilding Davison. Funerals are always political; the Chartists (mid-nineteenth-century radical reformers for the enfranchisement of the working class) and early trade unionists had already established the practice of merging funeral and political protest. The funeral in Manchester of Chartist activist Ernest Jones (1869) was the setting of the last Chartist rally. What is significant about Davison's funeral is that its overtly political nature was given a wider platform in a new era of mass communications, which merged the secular and the profane, the personal and the private. Although *The Times* was first published in the eighteenth century, it was the *Daily Telegraph* (1855) with its cover price of only a penny, affordable to the middle classes, and the introduction of mass circulation dailies for the working classes – *The People* (1881), *Daily Mail* (1896), *Daily Express* (1900), *Daily Mirror* (1903) – which established widespread newspaper readership by the Edwardian era.

The increasingly competitive market for newspapers led to greater sensationalism. W. T. Stead's exposure of child prostitution in 'Maiden Tribute to Modern Babylon', published in *The Pall Mall Gazette* in 1885, was an early example. Newspaper editors had a wide range of controversial stories to choose from in the Edwardian era: crime, poverty, deprivation, campaigns for home rule in Ireland, trade union agitation and the suffrage campaigns on behalf of approximately one-third of men and all women who, until the Representation of the People Act in 1918, were disenfranchised. By 1903, after many years of campaigning, some of the smaller women's suffrage groups – most notably Mrs Pankhurst's WSPU – frustrated by the slow progress of their cause, began to engage in a number of violent activities, disrupting public meetings or destroying property such as shop windows, which would ensure their arrest and newspaper coverage; arrests were often followed by hunger strikes, leading to forced feeding. WSPU activities were frequently seen on the front pages of newspapers and featured in the newsreels shown in the cinema, an emblem of twentieth-century modernity which by 1910 was a popular form of mass entertainment.

The media fascination with Davison's funeral was guaranteed by the circumstances which surrounded her death. The Derby was a key event in the Edwardian social calendar for all classes and was subject to considerable public attention, regularly filmed from the 1890s, and when Davison stepped on to the racecourse at Tattenham Corner on 4 June, she did so in front of a plethora of press and film cameras. The violent clash between Davison and the racehorses was thus a media event; the threat to horse and rider and the extent of Davison's injuries led to press speculation, often far from sympathetic, upon her sanity, motivations

Fig. 1 The procession at suffragette Emily Wilding Davison's funeral, London 1913. *Women's Library, London*

Fig. 2 Traffic is stopped as suffragette supporters follow the funeral cortège. *Women's Library, London*

Fig. 3 Young suffragettes dressed in white to symbolise purity. *Women's Library, London*

Fig. 4 Suffragettes stand guard at Emily Wilding Davison's coffin at Victoria Station. *Women's Library, London*

and the possibility of her survival until her death four days later. Debate raged then, and for many years afterwards, over whether Davison planned to die; the previous year she had attempted suicide when imprisoned in Holloway but had in her pocket at the Derby a return train ticket to London. An understanding of the interpretation of her death at the time needs to be framed by the knowledge that suicide was illegal and would have precluded a Christian burial and memorial service.

Politically, Davison's funeral and memorial service offered the WSPU the opportunity for a 'public display, bravado and a show of strength',[3] asserting to external observers the organisation's significance and respectability, whilst affirming for members and sympathisers a sense of community and belonging, and providing 'instruction and improvement' of the organisation's ideals.[4] The programme for the memorial ceremony, *The Suffragette* magazine and a speed-ily produced hagiography can be seen as the organisation's first attempts to control the narrative of Davison's life and death to serve their political aims. Davison was appropriated as a martyr for women's suffrage, whilst any inten-tion to commit suicide was denied and her action in grabbing the reins of the king's horse was presented as another unsuccessful petition to the king on behalf of women.

The WSPU at the time utilised religious imagery of angels and Joan of Arc, talked of their involvement in a 'Holy War' and littered the memorial programme with religious language and phrases, referring to Davison's 'noble sacrifice' and her 'laying down her life for others'. Arguably, religious discourse was and remains one of the most easily accessible and acceptable ways of expressing pas-sionately held views within western culture and hence is frequently drawn upon by secular political groups to instruct their followers and explain their actions to a wider public. The procession was a carefully choreographed visual specta-cle of melodramatic excess which accompanied the coffin to the church and back to King's Cross station for the coffin to be taken by train to Morpeth in Northumbria, where Davison's mother lived. Here she was buried after another procession. Detailed instructions to participants specified the flowers to be car-ried, their colour and the precise width of black armbands, and this all conveyed a sense of the organisation's unity and identity.

The procession was led by the hunger strikers and younger suffragettes who wore white dresses and were used on suffragette demonstrations to symbolise purity. They were also eminently suitable to construct strong iconic images in the black and white photography of the period, especially when juxtapo-sitioned against older WSPU members adorned in customary black funeral attire carrying purple irises, implying that death threatened purity and inno-cence. Cameras followed the procession, providing images for newspapers and cinemas across Britain and the world. A range of photographic postcards cap-tured significant moments of the melodrama: the coffin guarded by suffragettes at Victoria station or the funeral procession going round Piccadilly Circus.

The often unseen horror of the violence that women experienced in their fight for the suffrage – forced feeding, manhandling by police and Davison's death – were brought into the public sphere as women who, denied a voice in the parliamentary elections, appropriated the public space of the street – the funeral brought traffic to a halt.

Davison's hagiographer describes 'tears on the faces of many men who watched, gibes on lips of very few'.[5] Apparently occasional bricks were thrown at the coffin and whilst press coverage was not necessarily sympathetic, they reported the jockey's wife as one of the mourners. Although the WSPU could orchestrate media attention, they could not control the meanings and interpretations of the spectacle or narratives of Davison's life and death. Whilst the spectacle of mourning stimulated public debate, there is little evidence that it or Davison's death affected progress towards women's suffrage, which was caught up in machinations of party politics at Westminster.

Memorials, processions and funerals are only the beginning of the process of remembrance, which is fluid, shifting and contested. During the First World War, the Emily Davison Club, Lodge, pilgrimage and fellowship were set up to perpetuate and appropriate her memory. Through these organisations the notoriety of her martyrdom was aligned to pacifism and anti-imperialism; however, when Diane Atkinson, writing in the *New Statesman* (6/6/2005), suggested that there were links between Davison's actions and those of contemporary suicide bombers, responses were incredulous. For whilst suicide bombers are perceived as a threat to national security, in retrospect Davison's cause has been appropriated and legitimated; universal suffrage is associated with British national identity. Davison's grave has become a place of pilgrimage, with flowers laid on it, giving Morpeth a place on the tourist trail. In 2007 a Heritage Lottery Grant of £49,900 repaired the gravestone and developed an educational heritage experience for the numerous school children who study her life and activities.

The public funeral as a performance of sculptured remembrance in contemporary culture is now usually reserved for celebrities and dignitaries, but the political potential of media spectacles of public mourning, initially recognised by the WSPU, continues to offer dissident groups a political platform and publicity. At the height of the political troubles in Northern Ireland in the 1980s, IRA funerals were frequently highly performed events; the paramilitary masked men who accompanied the coffin and the volley of shots across the grave served to turn the event into a media spectacle and show of strength. More recently, the spectacle of coffins of repatriated soldiers from the Iraq and Afghanistan conflicts, draped in Union Jacks, unloaded from planes, passing through the Wiltshire market town of Wootton Basset and arriving at funerals, whilst expressing private grief, also create a plethora of media images which can be utilised to critique British government policy.

Notes

1   D. Mitchell, *The Fighting Pankhursts* (London: Jonathan Cape, 1976).

2   D.J. Pearsall, 'Burying the Duke: Victorian Mourning and the Funeral of the Duke of Wellington', *Victorian Literature and Culture*, Vol. 27 No 2 (1999).

3   A. Morley & L. Stanley, *The Life and Death of Emily Wilding Davison* (London: The Women's Press, 1988).

4   W. Godwin (1809), 'Essays on Sepulchres', quoted in P.A. Pickering & A. Tyrell, *Contested Sites: Commemoration, Memorial and Popular Politics in Nineteenth Century Britain* (Basingstoke: Ashgate, 2004).

5   G. Colmore, *The Life of Emily Wilding Davison* (1913); reprinted in A. Morley & L. Stanley, *The Life and Death of Emily Wilding Davison* (London: The Women's Press, 1988).

Thirty

'THEY TOOK MY HUSBAND, THEY TOOK THE MONEY AND JUST LEFT ME':

WAR WIDOWS & REMEMBRANCE AFTER THE SECOND WORLD WAR

Dr Janis Lomas

Remembrance in contemporary culture is intimately interwoven with the image of the grieving widow; however, the war widow as a separate and identifiable category only began in 1914 as a consequence of the large number of wives who lost their husbands in the first months of the war. Indeed, by the middle of 1915, no fewer than 128,401 war widows' pensions were being paid. After the First World War, although entitlement was difficult to establish, war widows were reasonably well looked after by the state. The pension was £1 a week for war widows under 40 without children and around £2 a week if you had one child. If you consider that unemployment benefit in the early 1930s paid only £1 9s 0d for a married couple and three children, you get some idea of the worth of the war widows' pension in the interwar years. It certainly was not generous but it was a reasonable amount. At the outbreak of war in September 1939, new war pension regulations were introduced. These new rates were considerably lower than those already being paid to First World War widows. Therefore, for the first four years of the Second World War these second-generation war widows were desperately poor and were treated substantially worse than those of the earlier war. This seemed to presage the treatment that Second World War widows were to receive. Although in July 1943 the pension rates for the two World Wars were finally assimilated to the existing rates for 1914–18 war widows, this increase left all war widows impoverished as the cost of living had risen by almost a third during the war years. The poverty war widows experienced then was to continue for decades. It eventually led to the formation of the War Widows' Association in 1971 and did not end until 1990, when the pension was finally substantially increased for most war widows.

In the post-war period, as the welfare state was gradually introduced, the war widow was seen as not being in need of any special treatment and William Beveridge, amongst others, called for an end to the distinction between a war widow and any other widowed woman. However, there were marked differences between the two categories. Not only was the state obligated to the family of a man who had died for his country, but the average age of a war widow was just 23 and many thousands had babies or very young children. They had not had the opportunity to take out insurance policies on the lives of their young husbands as insurance was not available to conscripts in the Second World War and they usually had little or no savings. In contrast, women widowed in the normal course of events had an average age of 60, their children were usually grown up and they often had some sort of pension, life insurance or savings.

In 1948, as part of the welfare state, National Assistance was introduced. This provision enabled successive governments to keep war pension provision low. As H.A. Marquand, the Minister of Pensions, wrote to the British Legion in 1949:

> I fully appreciate and deeply sympathise with the plight of the war widow, but I need hardly remind you that a war widow in need is now eligible for assistance from the National Assistance Board.[1]

The number of war widows forced to ask for National Assistance rose steadily. By 1957 the figure was around 3,000 and it was to remain around this level for the next two decades. However, many war widows in desperate need refused to claim National Assistance. As National Assistance was means tested they associated it with charity, the Poor Law and parish relief. Officers of the Ministry of Pensions also continued to make value judgements in much the same way as charitable workers and Poor Law Guardians had in the past. As one war widow wrote:

> When I was in the Pensions Office, the Clerical officer said: 'Have you only one child?' I said 'Yes', he replied 'Good thing the Government is paying out enough for you war widows'.[2]

There was only one increase in war widows' pension rates between 1946 and 1955. The consistent poverty this war widow describes is typical:

> I used to get the pension on a Monday and by Thursday there was nothing left, nowhere to go, no help … I used to allow myself a penny a day for the gas, I used to bath the children and put them to bed, then I used to go to bed to save the light. If I bought a loaf of bread and a pot of jam one day, the next day I had to economise.[3]

In the post-war economic circumstances, as employment opportunities for women gradually opened up, war widows were expected to earn their own living. At least one MP saw distinct advantages for widows in going out to work. During a debate in the House of Commons, Douglas Houghton MP was reported as having said:

> The best thing that can happen to most widows is that they should get married again; and the best chance they have of that is to go out into the world and meet men – they are more likely to do that at work than they are by sitting at home waiting for the milkman.[4]

This rather callous remark seems indicative of the dismissive attitude which many war widows felt was commonplace after the war. Only war widows with children were viewed as needing support, hence the lack of any increase in the pension paid to childless war widows under 40, whose pension remained unchanged at £1 for forty-eight years from 1919–67.[5]

War widows were often ill-equipped to earn a living, had little prospect of any training and were grieving deeply after the loss of a young husband. Many war widows with children could only manage part-time work in addition to their domestic responsibilities; however, this left them much more vulnerable to dismissal as they were often used to cover temporary fluctuations in demand and were also exempt from redundancy payments. In their social relations there remained an onus on war widows to be respectable. Although not publicised at the time, the Ministry of Pensions continued with the removal of the war widows' pension from women who were considered 'unworthy' because of cohabitation, immorality or child neglect in exactly the same way as had been enforced during and after the First World War.[6]

By 1948, an additional 153,426 women had been awarded a war widows' pension. In the years following the Second World War, the pension differential between a woman widowed in the normal course of events and a war widow narrowed to as little as 6s. The meagre level of pension provision available and the change in ideology and perception meant that, despite the introduction of the welfare state, war widows both during and after the Second World War were significantly worse off than during the interwar years. In 1957, the British Legion found that in order to restore the worth of the war widows' pension to what it had been in 1938, it would have to be increased by almost a third. The women who suffered the greatest financial difficulties fell into three main groups: firstly, those whose husbands were permanently disabled, either physically or mentally, by the war. Secondly, those war widows who were left with young children to bring up alone. These younger war widows had little choice but to find paid work despite any domestic commitments they might have. They also had to pay income tax on their war widows' pensions at the 'unearned income' rate, which often left them with as little as 4s remaining from their pension after tax was paid. The only war pension to be taxed was the war widows' pension. Disabled male war pensioners received their war pension tax free. A sizeable number of war widows put their children into foster care or up for adoption because of the desperate conditions they found themselves in. The third group who suffered greatly were First World War widows. They were particularly hard hit as they were reaching middle or old age when the value of their pension diminished, and they found it increasingly difficult to subsidise their pension by paid work because of their advancing age. Many of these widows were still going out to work in their eighties.

In 1971 war widows decided they'd had enough of the treatment they had received from successive governments and formed the War Widows' Association to fight for their rights. They fought a long hard battle which lasted until 1990, when, at long last, war widows began to receive a more reasonable pension and almost all the anomalies in their treatment were gradually addressed. However, the difficulties experienced by these women is a reminder that the legacy of war and the spirit of remembrance must always address the physical, psychological and financial needs of all those who suffer as a result of war and conflict.

Notes

1 Public Record Office, Ministry of Pensions PIN59/50, letter to British Legion, 10 May 1949.

2 J. Lomas, War Widows' Questionnaire reply, M.N.

3 C. Kirton, *Open Space*, BBC2, November 1987. The quotation which forms part of the title of this chapter is derived from the same source.

4 Staffordshire University, War Widows' Archive, Box 11. This newspaper cutting is unfortunately undated but the incensed war widow who had kept the cutting stated that it dated from 1942 or 1943 and originated in the *Daily Mail*.

5 Many war widows felt that both successive governments and the general public displayed indifference towards them after 1945. For war widows with children and for those over 40, the pension paid in 1945 was 32 6d, with an extra 11s for each child. This was very low when compared with the average wage of a male manual worker, which was, in July 1945, £6 1s 4d. The war widows' pension was increased by 2s 6d per week in February 1946, but then remained the same, at 35s for the next six years. The child allowance remained at 11s for eleven years from 1944–55, by which time the wages of the average male manual worker had risen to £11 7s 10d.

6 J. Lomas, '"Delicate Duties": Issues of class and respectability in government policy towards the wives and widows of British soldiers in the era of the Great War', *Women's History Review*, Vol. 9 No 1 (2000).

Thirty-one

REMEMBERING WOMEN:
Envisioning More Inclusive War Remembrance in Twenty-First-Century Britain

Dr Debra Marshall

Remembering women's wartime activities in Great Britain has roots in our ancient history. School children still learn about Boudicca, Queen of the Iceni, probably the earliest and best-known example of a woman warrior in the British Isles. But her story is indicative of how public memory ebbs and flows in accordance with the prevailing mood of the times. Boudicca's uprising against the occupying Romans in *c.* AD 60–61 was important enough to be recorded by the Roman historian Tacitus, but then she was forgotten, until being rediscovered during the fifteenth century. Memory faded again until the Victorian era, when her story so captured the public imagination that Queen Victoria was being portrayed as the warrior queen in paintings. A bronze statue of Boudicca and her daughters in her war chariot (by Thomas Thornycroft) was unveiled in 1905 and still stands today next to Westminster Bridge and the Houses of Parliament. Since then, the memory of Boudicca has had brief, periodic revivals but she is currently no longer the subject of much public interest. This reminds us that remembrance is a process and that active participation by the public both creates and sustains it.

In spite of Boudicca's example, a strong sense of societal discomfort at associating women with war – either as warriors themselves or as victims of war – has prevailed for much of British history. Although attitudes have gradually changed, and increasing numbers of women are serving in the armed forces on the front line, these historical attitudes have limited the opportunities available to women and have thus influenced when and where we have remembered their wartime contributions.

Fig. 1 First World War Empire Memorial commemorative oak screen, York Minster.

Women in their millions contributed to the First World War effort – as members of the Women's Royal Air Force, the Women's Land Army, the Women's Forage Corps, as doctors, nurses and munitions workers, as well as by taking on jobs previously done by men. Their efforts were commemorated in 1923 when 32,000 members of the public subscribed to the appeal to create what was described at the time as the world's first war memorial to women. The money collected from women throughout Britain was used to restore an important thirteenth-century stained-glass window in York Minster and to install a commemorative oak screen.

The names of 1,465 women from the British Empire, who had died as a consequence of their involvement in the war effort, were listed behind the screen doors. The memorial was inaugurated on 25 July 1925 by the then Duchess of York, the late Queen Mother; the event was widely reported in the newspapers both nationally and internationally. Although the memorial was described as the 'national' women's cenotaph, this role never gained wide public recognition and over time its status as the national memorial for women has been largely unac-

Fig. 2 Marquette of proposed memorial to the women of the Second World War.

knowledged. Along with other memorials in the vicinity, it was and still is of interest to visitors to the minster, but it is generally unknown to the wider public. Indeed, many of the women commemorated by this memorial have passed into virtual obscurity, with the exception of some individuals, Edith Cavell perhaps being the most notable, who continue to receive public recognition.

What is surprising is that this memorial did not provide inspiration for the women who were instrumental in the creation of the most recent national memorial to women. The idea for the new memorial was originally raised at a reunion of ex-servicewomen in York, many of whom were aware of the First World War memorial in York Minster. Although proposed by ex-servicewomen, the memorial's constituency was quickly expanded to include all women who had contributed to the war effort. This created some tensions and difficulties – some felt this diluted the action-oriented roles of the ex-servicewomen by associating them with civilians. Another issue for many of the ex-servicewomen was their feeling that the limitations of age – lack of mobility, health issues and disconnectedness from internet communication – placed limits on their ability to tap into a wider constituency. This contrasts with the earlier memorial whose supporters could draw on an international network of women's associations.

They were, however, zealous fundraisers and, having secured the £1 million needed for the memorial, they turned their attention to the form the memorial would take and its location. In order to reach a wide audience, memorials must usually occupy a prominent position in a landscape with nationally recognised cultural significance. In this instance this is limited to a single location – Whitehall – the site of the Cenotaph and the national war remembrance ceremony on Remembrance Sunday. Since the women's memorial was to be a national memorial, nothing less than a place in London was considered appropriate, and although other options were mooted, Whitehall was always the first choice. This aim to secure a highly visible location for the memorial contrasts strongly with the form and location of the earlier Women's Empire Memorial in a dark corner of York Minster.

When the design for the new memorial was revealed in the press it caused outrage. Following a selection process, two internationally renowned sculptors had been asked to combine their individual designs to form a composite sculpture.

The proposed memorial (see Fig. 2) comprised a figure of a woman in bronze, taken from a Second World War photograph of an air-raid precaution warden, who was sheltering children from a bomb blast with her body. On the stone plinth below carvings of clothes – hats, bags and coats hanging on pegs – were intended to illustrate the range of jobs carried out by women during the war. Although most of the women I spoke with about the design strongly preferred a figurative memorial, the majority were unhappy about the choice of what they felt was a passive representation of their active participation in the war. They wanted their active wartime roles, such as drivers, height-finders and mechanics, to be shown graphically and not symbolically by the clothing they wore. One woman commented that the empty clothing reminded her of 'missing bodies' and felt that the clothing could have as easily belonged to men as to women. The few women who were not upset by the use of clothing were dissatisfied by their association with an image of maternal sacrifice. In later life many of them had indeed become mothers, but it was their younger wartime selves who had been active in the service of their country and should be represented by the memorial.

After this publicity the Memorial Committee faced a barrage of letters strongly criticising the proposed design; some women demanded back their donations. In response to this disapproval, the original design was modified to remove the top part of the sculpture. This left the plinth with the reliefs of clothing, and although this part of the memorial had also drawn criticism, it had been less ferocious than that directed at the figures. Faced with a memorial half the size of the original design, John Mills, the sculptor responsible for its lower part, elongated the plinth in an attempt to restore its proportions. The redesigned memorial now had a strong resemblance to the iconic Cenotaph, albeit with

Fig. 3 Memorial to the Women of World War II, Whitehall, London.

clothes attached. After much lobbying over planning permission, many setbacks and further delays, the application for a site 75m from the Cenotaph in Whitehall was successful. The Memorial to the Women of World War II was inaugurated on 9 July 2004 in Whitehall, London. Intended as the national memorial recognising the contributions of all British women during the Second World War, it is unusual in commemorating the lives rather than the deaths of these women.

Although the form of the earlier York memorial is more chameleon-like, blending into the fabric of the building more than its freestanding sister memorial in Whitehall, the women commemorated in York are named and this holds out the possibility that research could reveal more about their lives and deaths. The Memorial to the Women of World War II carries no names, and because of women's under-representation on other memorials, the threat to memory this poses has been recognised. A plaque on the memorial states its purpose and directs readers to an archive at the Imperial War Museum containing personal accounts of women's wartime experiences. However, this will only be useful as long as the archive continues to exist.

Although the memorial is co-located with the Cenotaph in Whitehall, it has not been incorporated into the Remembrance Sunday commemorations, but this proximity has drawn media comment during the parade and so the public is made aware of its existence and purpose. This may prove vital for the survival of its role as long-term carrier of public memory.

In spite of their differences, what these memorials have in common is that they are a testament to the active role played by women in the service of their country. They remind us of the changes to women's roles in society, of their moving into the public eye from behind closed doors, from being concealed and inward-looking in the case of the First World War memorial in York Minster, to being remembered in Whitehall, the single most important site in British national war remembrance. The changes in the social, political and cultural conditions of the twentieth century impacted on women's lives and consequently, the remembrance of those lives and changes in the twenty-first century will also leave their imprint. British women have moved from participating in war remembrance, largely as mourners of men, to claiming recognition for their own contribution. They have orchestrated the building of war memorials to remember women, campaigned for public acknowledgement of their wartime contribution and losses, and are increasingly taking part in acts of public remembrance. This recognition has taken time and it was only in 2000, more than half a century after the end of the Second World War, that the Women's Land Army and the Women's Timber Corps joined other veterans in the annual Remembrance Sunday parade past the Cenotaph for the first time.

Yet as the disconnections between these national memorials show, the tradition has tensions and blind spots. The past does not always sustain the present. Who participates and who is included in commemorative activities changes over time and is as much about today and our vision of the future as it is about yesterday. To make remembrance sustainable it seems clear that those who inherit and carry on the tradition will have to be prepared to take on the priorities and conflicts of new generations. A more inclusive tradition will be better equipped to meet new challenges, and a tradition with an increased number of female participants and more reflective of wider society contains the promise that remembrance may be more indicative of the contribution of not only British women, but all who serve their country in their different ways in future years. Whilst the meaning of our memorials is created and sustained by acts of remembrance, it is the will to remember that will renew the tradition and keep it alive for future generations.

Memorials Across the World

THE final section provides an interesting comparison between the kinds of remembrance prevalent in UK culture with that of other countries. While some of the examples are drawn from countries where the UK has had a cultural influence, such as South Africa and the USA, in Rwanda at the Resistance Memorial at Bisesero, an innovative example of the inter-relationship between remembrance and reconciliation has emerged. In the end, exploring remembrance across cultures helps to provide a degree of some understanding of the distinction between the universal and the more narrowly cultural aspects of remembrance.

Thirty-two

STIGMATA OF STONE:
MONUMENTS, MEMORIALS & MARKERS IN THE US LANDSCAPE

Professor Susan-Mary Grant

The United States of America is a nation born, as most are, in conflict, but not just military conflict; as a nation comprising indigenous and immigrant, both voluntary and involuntary, it has witnessed many battles over representation of who belongs in the nation, whose history, in effect, the land reflects, whose story the memorials on that landscape tell, whose memories they invoke and whose identity they assert. Yet memorials, by their nature, speak to loss; they set in stone a relationship between the past and the present, the living and the dead, not just the dead of war, but frequently victims of violence, natural disasters or man-made tragedies. Memorials can also, however, either evoke or challenge a particular interpretation of such events; they can be commemorative but simultaneously corrective; they can assert agency and force hidden, if hardly forgotten, aspects of the nation's history into public consciousness.

Both personal and political remembrance culture in the USA encompasses far more than the sacrifice of the nation's warriors, and stretches far beyond the Mall in Washington DC. From the burial grounds of the eighteenth century to Ground Zero in the twenty-first; and from the Montebello Genocide Memorial in California to the Space Mirror (Astronaut) Memorial in the grounds of the John F. Kennedy Space Center in Florida, the nation's commemorative landscape – one that extends beyond the geography of the nation state itself – reflects a global response to remembrance, to human ambition, to loss and to the need to preserve, in physical form, the memories that collectively symbolise the nation. Nevertheless, the development of physical memorials in the USA should not be taken for granted.

Fig. 1 The Tripoli Naval Monument, unveiled in 1807, as it appeared on the western terrace of the US Capitol, Washington DC, in the mid-nineteenth century. It was moved to the Naval Academy, Annapolis, Maryland in 1860. *Library of Congress Prints and Photographs Division (LC-USZ62-86368)*

Consciously founded as a new republic, repudiating Old World social, political, religious and indeed commemorative structures and forms, the population of the early United States perceived physical memorials signifying anything more than an individual death as antithetical to its republican creed. Even the commemorative culture surrounding the American War of Independence did not really develop until much later in the nineteenth century. One of the earliest commemorative forms to appear outside of a burial ground was war related but not, in any sense, a commemoration of conflict in a national context. Privately commissioned and funded, the monument to sailors who perished during the

Fig. 2 A detail from the bronze relief on the South Carolina African American History Monument depicting the passage of what became known as 'Brown vs. Board of Education' (1954), the Supreme Court case that ended legal segregation in the nation's schools. This had been, in fact, five separate cases, hence the reference to one of the others; a corrective of, as well as a call, to memory. *Author's Collection*

Tripolitan (Barbary) War (see Fig. 1) was the expression of one man's desire to acknowledge the sacrifice of comrades in a war that few acknowledged at the time and which has been all but forgotten since. Indeed, so far from a memorial to the dead, the Tripolitan Monument was swiftly transmuted, for public consumption, as signifying the birth of the US navy.

It was the American Civil War of 1861–65 that instigated an upsurge in physical monuments and memorials in the USA – not merely the proliferation of monuments to the nation's military leaders and to the dead, but, after 1865, of monuments of every type after an inevitable process of accretion occurred. Inevitably, as soon as one regiment or one town had a memorial, most others followed suit. On a deeper level, however, this intensive period of memorial construction also reflected the inevitable reassessment of the nation and its meaning that the Civil War had prompted. For the states of the former Confederacy, monuments represented not just a response to the grief produced by the loss of individual lives, and the defeat of a putative national life, but a quiet continuation of the rebellion itself. Forced into silence on the subject of secession from the nation, the former Confederacy allowed mute stone to speak for it; and it spoke volumes. Across the south, in town squares and in memorial parks, white southerners established their marker on a nation that would, until well into the twentieth century, be informed by their racial perspective.

The Confederate challenge to the nation's very existence, of course, established a contrary commemorative culture, one devoted to retaining (often this has meant retrieving) the memory of what the Civil War had been about; not just the survival of a nation, but the eradication of chattel slavery within that nation. Not until 1954 did segregation in the south begin to come under legislative attack, and not until 2001 was a monument erected in Columbia, South Carolina, to commemorate the demise of slavery and segregation (see Fig. 2). Such a monument, at the heart of the state that led the south out of the Union in 1861, is a particularly potent assertion of African American agency, as well as a sober reminder of the many thousands of slaves who had suffered under the south's 'peculiar institution'. It is a monument of many parts, including a large slab engraved with the routes that the slave ships took to North America, four rocks from their places of departure (Senegal, Sierra Leone, Ghana and the Congo) and a detailed bronze relief depicting African American history in the United States. Positioned at the crossroads of slavery and freedom, secession and nationalism, the South Carolina monument represents the use of the monument to assert both agency and presence in a nation too ready, at times, to deny both to African Americans.

What really distinguishes the African American history monument from other forms of commemoration, particularly war commemoration, is its deliberately universal, national representation. No individual is identified on this monument; no names of civil rights leaders – although that might have been expected. In part, this draws attention to the fact that although slavery represented the sacrifice of

Fig. 3 One of the commemorative statues in the Cambridge American Military Cemetery which is devoted to the dead of the Second World War. Maintained by the American Battle Monuments Commission, it was a temporary cemetery from 1943 onwards and a permanent memorial after 1956. *Author's Collection*

many thousands of lives, most of these are and always will be anonymous. In other respects, although the USA, like the UK, has at the heart of the nation a Tomb to the Unknown Soldier of the First World War, the anonymous monument in the United States tends to represent a site of tragedy outside the context of military conflict; yet conflict itself is often a constant.

The erection of a monument, indeed, is by no means a guarantor of memory, nor of permanence. An example is the monument raised to commemorate the police after the Haymarket Riot on 4 May 1886. Controversy has always surrounded this event, where the police fired into a demonstration of striking workers, resulting in the deaths of several policemen and strikers alike. In this case, the monument became a focus, as most are, but not one that assuaged grief; more one that inspired anger. In the years that followed its dedication in 1888, it was vandalised and had a street car driven into it. On several occasions attempts were made to blow it up, and at least two of these, in 1969 and 1970, were successful. A locus of public frustration, first in the immediate context of the original riot and later in the context of demonstrations against the war in Vietnam, the statue was eventually moved to the police academy. Its violent history, played out time and again for the duration of its period of public display, rendered it entirely inappropriate as a public marker of sacrifice, since those whom it commemorated were not understood to have been acting in the public interest; the monument to them, therefore, failed in its function as a memorial site.

The reaction to the Haymarket monument was an extreme example of the contentious nature of commemorative culture in the USA. Since the nation's inception, the struggle between memory and forgetting, whether the event or issue in question is a war, a natural disaster, an institution such as slavery or a class struggle such as at Haymarket, has frequently been intense. The USA has always felt on safer commemorative ground when that ground is not located within the nation and the audience not wholly citizens of the USA. In the American cemeteries of Europe that were constructed after both World Wars (see Fig. 3), an apparently more straightforward memorial message is conveyed, one that asks those outside the USA to contemplate the sacrifices made by that nation in the salvation of their own. This is not a message that all Europeans feel comfortable with. Even here, perhaps especially here, the contentious nature of commemoration for the USA remains one to contemplate in the twenty-first century.

Thirty-three

THE RESISTANCE MEMORIAL, BISESERO, RWANDA

Dr Rachel Ibreck

The Resistance Memorial in Rwanda is a national monument to the bravery of the Tutsis who fought back against the 1994 genocide in the hills of Bisesero. Their suffering and courage have since drawn international attention, yet the memorial was a local initiative, like the resistance it commemorates. It was created to honour the victims and to ease the grief felt by the few survivors and it is associated with efforts to repair social relations within a divided community.[1]

The memorial is built on a massacre site; the death toll in Bisesero was huge, a devastating episode in a genocide that ended in close to a million deaths in a period of three months. Tutsis began to be hunted down and killed across Rwanda on 7 April 1994. In the days that followed, many fled to the hills of Bisesero from the surrounding region of Kibuye, seeking refuge in this mountainous area with the local Abasesero Tutsis. Up to 50,000 people are thought to have hidden in the forests and among the rocks in this rural landscape.[2] They faced repeated attacks from well-armed militiamen, soldiers, local officials and civilians, but fought back under the leadership of a group of Abasesero men, who used their hilltop location to their advantage. The fighting continued for weeks with deaths on both sides until 13 May, when the supporters of genocide returned with reinforcements, massacring thousands. By June, the resistance had collapsed: most of the refugees were dead and the few survivors were in hiding, overcome with exhaustion. There was a brief moment of hope, when soldiers stopped in Bisesero on 26 June, part of *Opération Turquoise* – a French-led military force sent in a belated attempt to establish a 'safe zone'. The remaining refugees appealed for protection but were abandoned and endured a final onslaught the

Fig. 1 The approach to Bisesero's Resistance Memorial, Rwanda.

following day. When the French returned in July to evacuate them, there were only around 1,000 survivors.[3]

Work on the memorial began two years after the genocide. The surviving Abasasero had returned to the hills where they found the skulls and bones of genocide victims either lying on the hillside or in shallow pits. Like survivors from other massacres in Rwanda, they searched for the dead and sought ways to rebury and remember them. They gained support from a survivors' association, Kibuye Solidarity, in 1996. In 1998, Vedaste Ngarambe, an architect from the region who lost close and extended family in the massacres, proposed a monument for Bisesero and was awarded a grant from the Ministry of Youth, Sports and Culture to create it. His hope was that a memorial would settle the 'agitated spirits' of the dead and help survivors to bear their sorrow; the idea was born out of personal grief and an understanding of the collective anguish of the bereaved.[4]

When the memorial was conceived, there was still conflict between the surviving Tutsis and Hutus living nearby. The survivors suspected their Hutu neighbours, among whom were militiamen who participated in the violence and their families. The Hutus also had reason to fear the trauma of the victims – the Abasesero had proved themselves as combatants, during and prior to the genocide, countering attacks on Tutsis in Bisesero in 1959, 1962 and 1973. Despite their hostility, both groups were persuaded to help build the memorial on the basis that 'co-habitation is necessary'. The architect was a Tutsi who

Fig. 2 The path of remembrance in Bisesero, Rwanda.

fought for the Rwandan Patriotic Army against the genocidal regime in 1994. He employed a Hutu mason, conscripted prisoners accused of genocide and paid local people to work on the site, including survivors. All participated 'according to their strength, women and men', the local councillor recalled.[5]

Through the construction of the Resistance Memorial survivors inscribed their memories of genocide on the mountainous landscape. The monument was designed as a place of mourning and education. At the base of the monument is a tribute to the fighters, and a record of their hollow victory in an inverted 'arc of triumph'. Nearby is a sculpture, a stone surrounded by spears – the weapons the Tutsis used in their defence. Further on is a hexagonal edifice, like a small tomb; here visitors pause to survey the hillside and decide whether to proceed. The memorial involves a demanding journey – a metaphoric struggle for survival. The visitor must climb steep steps up the hillside – a test of endurance. They are surrounded by walls, high at the beginning, to represent a lack of liberty and knowledge, but diminishing by the end, when the truth of the genocide is known. Along the way are paths in diverse directions and obstacles preventing flight. Wild fruit grows as a reminder that the environment was the sole source of aid for the refugees: 'nature nourished and remained faithful to them, more than man.' This journey represents the 'spiral of suffering, the physical grief' experienced by the victims. It leads to nine houses, each representing an area of Kibuye, where the bones of the dead are to be displayed. At

Fig. 3 Overlooking the Resistance Memorial from the 'summit of hope', Rwanda.

the summit of the hill is a vast concrete burial chamber surrounded by the trees which gave shelter during the genocide, and by new trees, planted to represent the individuals who died. The 'summit of hope' is a place to remember and mourn loved ones.

The trauma of the genocide defines the survivor community in Bisesero and cements their relationship with the memorial; survivors are often at the site. But remembrance cannot overcome the legacy of suffering, and it is fraught with difficulties. Among these is a lack of funds to maintain and finish the memorial and a need to resolve the issue of the remains of a thousand victims: skulls and bones kept in a shed at the base of the site for a decade, awaiting preservation and display. There are also tensions arising from the genocide: the survivors' will to remember is not shared by all the people of Bisesero – local Hutus rarely visit.

Nevertheless, the creation of the memorial was a practical step towards better community relations which gave purpose and relief to survivors. Its architect spoke of how the memorial 'healed' him, giving him a place to grieve and find consolation. He believes that working together to build the monument helped people on both sides of the community; such initiatives, he said, are essential as a 'remedy against genocide'. He spoke of steps towards justice and forgiveness and positive examples of economic and social interaction, including marriages between survivors and Hutu women.

The memorial is implicated in a fragile co-existence between survivors and their Hutu neighbours. Each year, during national genocide commemorations, all local residents are called to participate. A young woman survivor from a nearby village admitted she is wary of Hutus, but that going with them to the memorial in Bisesero during the commemoration 'helps' her to live alongside them: 'They call people with the drum. Hutu and Tutsi together walk to the summit … We welcomed them.' A convicted genocide perpetrator, who confessed to involvement in the killing of his neighbours' children, is among those committed to making this ritual journey: 'The memorial really touches me. We will participate in commemoration until the end of our days.'[6]

The Resistance Memorial has altered the scenery and the pattern of survivors' lives in Bisesero. Rising from a plateau where the Abasasero have rebuilt their homes, it is at the centre of their daily existence and is a means by which they endure their loss. They live close to the dead and have become the guardians of memory, watching over the site and regularly making the arduous climb to the summit. Its meaning for survivors was described by a local councillor who lost many relatives and five children in the massacres: 'For this community, to remember is an obligation. The monument is important because it gives value to people … It matters for humanity. The grandeur of the monument gives worth to human dignity.'

Notes

1   This chapter is based on the author's research trips to the memorial site in Bisesero in August 2006 and April 2007, including interviews with local residents. For background on the 1994 genocide, see G. Prunier, *The Rwanda Crisis: History of a Genocide* (London: Hurst & Co., 2nd revised edn, 1998).

2   This estimate of those who fled and died here is used officially and at the International Criminal Tribunal for Rwanda (ICTR), but it may be lower; see P. Verwimp, 'A Quantitative Analysis of Genocide in Kibuye Prefecture, Rwanda', *Development Economics Center for Economic Studies Discussions Paper Series* (DPS) 01.10 (2001), p. 22.

3   For a detailed account of the massacre, see African Rights, *Resisting Genocide: Bisesero, April–June 1994* (London: African Rights, 1997). Six of the leading perpetrators were convicted of genocide at the ICTR; see ICTR, 2010 [www.unictr.org/tabid/173/Default.aspx], accessed on 24/8/2010.

4   Interview with Vedaste Ngarambe, August 2006.

5   Interview with Bisesero councillor, April 2007.

6   Interviews in Mubuga, April 2007. The perpetrator had been imprisoned and served a reduced sentence following his confession.

Thirty-four

CONSTITUTION HILL, JOHANNESBURG:

BUILDING DEMOCRACY ON REMEMBRANCE

Dr Tony King

The newly developed site of Constitution Hill sits on the spot of the Old Fort prison complex in central Johannesburg. As a site it combines the new Constitutional Court with spaces for heritage areas and relevant bodies dedicated to human rights, and is intended as an open public space in a city characterised more by the legacy of segregation. Its purpose is not to erase traces of iniquity, but to appropriate them as part of building the emblematic landscape of democratic South Africa. The court was established after the fall of apartheid and the advent of democracy in 1994. It is South Africa's highest court, charged with interpreting the post-apartheid Constitution and upholding the Bill of Rights, and is a crucial institution of South Africa's young democracy.

A prison for ninety years until 1983, the Fort and other penal buildings on the site over the years held a cross-section of South African society: Boer commanders in the 1899–1902 South African War; striking white miners in the 1920s; political prisoners of all races; common criminals; and hundreds of thousands of ordinary black South Africans who were caught in the web of racist laws that comprised apartheid. It developed as a segregated prison complex. The Old Fort was for white men; Number Four and the Awaiting Trial Block (ATB) for black men; the Women's Gaol was mixed race but segregated. It was the prison for central Johannesburg, and has sometimes been compared to Robben Island, the prison island off Cape Town that held prominent political prisoners.

Originally on the edge of town atop the gold-bearing reef whose wealth has shaped South African history and society, the Old Fort was quickly surrounded by the expanding city. By the 1960s it was squeezed between built-up Hillbrow

Fig. 1 Events at Constitution Hill.

Fig. 2 ATB stairwell as part of the Constitutional Court foyer, with original graffiti: *Viva MK* – 'Long live MK' (MK was the armed wing of the African National Congress).

Fig. 3 The Constitutional Court's exterior in all eleven official languages.

and the business district of Braamfontein. It was overlooked by whites-only residential high-rises and municipal offices, as well as a nurses' home attached to a whites-only women's hospital. Its courtyards, where black prisoners (never white prisoners) were stripped and humiliated, were therefore in public view.

In 1998, after fifteen years of neglect, the Old Fort complex was chosen as the site of the new Constitutional Court, as well as related institutions concerned with human rights, and a heritage precinct comprising several former prison buildings. The intention was for appropriate commercial development to also take place on part of the site, but plans for this have stalled. The Constitutional Court building was completed in 2004, and interpretive and museum spaces are functioning. The only prison building not to survive was the ATB, on whose footprint the court now stands, although its stairwells were retained and have been integrated into the design of the court itself and the open area outside it, and its bricks were used for the walls of the court chamber. By recognising the diversity of the incarcerated, Constitution Hill seeks to neutralise the divisions that are apparent in modern South Africa. Therefore, it seeks to be representative of South African society, and to resonate with people of all backgrounds, most of all with black South Africans. There are exhibitions for Nelson Mandela and Mahatma Gandhi, for the Old Fort was the only prison in the world to have held them both. Other exhibitions recount the stories of political and ordinary prisoners who were approached to weave the narrative when the court was being built.

But Constitution Hill remembers most of all the hundreds of thousands of black South Africans held there; detained or convicted by the racist apartheid laws that criminalised their everyday life. The Heritage, Education and Tourism team that set up the heritage spaces at Constitution undertook extensive interviews with former prisoners in order to both shape the displays and to give former prisoners a stake in the site's new purpose. In that regard, it is very different from Robben Island and does not fall neatly into a linear liberation struggle narrative. Because it was an everyday prison, the banality of evil that it represents is more firmly rooted in the lived experience of ordinary South Africans. That mundanity arguably makes it a fitting site for the Constitutional Court, whose jurisdiction extends over all South Africans without favour.

The interpretation areas reflect the mixture of political and common prisoners, emphasising that the vast majority who passed through Number Four and the Women's Gaol were victims of an unfair judicial system. The display in Cell Two at Number Four, 'Who is a Criminal?', consists of photographs of anonymous prisoners that challenges the viewer to ponder the crimes and the reality of incarceration for black men. The Women's Gaol especially draws attention to the different regimes white and black prisoners encountered in prison.

However, the great leader narrative is not absent. Mandela's cell in the Fort has been turned into a display area. The Gandhi display in Number Four draws a linear narrative of resistance to oppression, linking South Africa to other struggle mainstreams, and emphasising the contrast between violent state oppression and non-violent defiance (South African liberation movements did not practice non-violence, but did subordinate violent action to diplomacy, civil disobedience and moral campaigning). Gandhi himself had developed his philosophy of non-violence in South Africa in the late nineteenth century.

Every part of Constitution Hill has been conceived as an interpretation area. The 360-degree rampart walk, now complete, makes use of the Hill's position on the reef, simultaneously above the city and yet overlooked by high-rises, thus placing the experience of incarceration at the centre of daily urban life. In the court building itself, much space is given over to the court's internationally acclaimed art collection of South African artists, especially struggle art, some of it repatriated or saved from obscurity. The sharpest reminder of where the Old Fort complex was, and how far it has transformed, is in the court foyer, where a preserved ATB stairwell is incorporated into the design, and on it survives the graffito 'Viva MK'.

Constitution Hill creates a bridge between the authoritarianism and democracy, oppression and liberation, division and unity. By showing how brutal the past was it emphasises how important human rights and democracy are, and by appropriating a former prison it emphasises the journey that South Africa has taken from tyranny to democracy. As well as the Constitutional Court, there are already a few Chapter 9 bodies (named after the chapter in the Bill of Rights that established them to protect human rights) on site. The eventual ambition is for Constitution Hill to become a human rights campus with a host of related bodies on site. For now, it is a high-profile heritage site in Johannesburg that draws thousands of visitors each month. Many of those are schoolchildren being educated on where they have come from, especially as the anti-apartheid struggle begins to move from living memory to history. Inmates approaching release from nearby prisons are brought here to take part in workshops on citizenship, turning the site's purpose neatly on its head.

Constitution Hill has appropriated the past to build the future. It has taken a place of oppression and detention and turned it into the country's highest court as well as a heritage site dedicated to the narrative of human rights. Therefore, unlike other sites, it does not carry out its nation-building remit simply through static museums and heritage areas. By hosting the Constitutional Court and related bodies, it places itself firmly in the structures of post-apartheid South Africa.

Further Reading

M. Gevisser (2004), From the ruins: the Constitution Hill project, *Public Culture*, 16 (3), 507–19

B. Law-Viljoen (2008), *Art and Justice: The Art of the Constitutional Court of South Africa*, Johannesburg: David Krut Publishing

—— (2006), *Light on a Hill: Building the Constitutional Court of South Africa*, Johannesburg: David Krut Publishing

C. Madikida, L. Segal & C. van den Berg (2008), *The Reconstruction of Memory at Constitution Hill*, The Public Historian, 30 (1), 17–25

L. Segal (2006), *Number Four: the making of Constitution Hill*, London: Penguin

L. Segal, C. van den Berg & C. Madikida (2007), *Mapping Memory: former prisoners tell their stories*, Johannesburg: David Krut Publishing

INDEX